Lifegivers

Framing the Birthparent Experience in Open Adoption

By James L. Gritter

CWLA Press

Washington, DC

CWLA Press is an imprint of the Child Welfare League of America (CWLA). The nation's oldest and largest membership-based child welfare organization, CWLA is committed to engaging all Americans in promoting the well-being of children and protecting every child from harm.

© 2000 Child Welfare League of America, Inc.

CHILD WELFARE LEAGUE OF AMERICA, INC.
440 First Street NW, Third Floor, Washington DC 20001-2085
E-mail: books@cwla.org

CURRENT PRINTING (last digit)
10 9 8 7 6 5 4 3 2 1

Cover design by Luke Johnson
Text design by Steve Boehm

Printed in the United States of America
ISBN # 0–87868–770–X

Library of Congress Cataloging-in-Publication Data

Gritter, James L., 1950–
    Lifegivers : framing the birthparent experience in open adoption / by
    James L. Gritter.
      p. cm.
    Includes bibliographical references.
    ISBN 0-87868-770-X (alk. paper)
      1. Open adoption--United States. 2. Birthparents--United States. I.
    Child Welfare League of America. II. Title.

HV875.55 .G74 2000
362.73'4'0973--dc21
                                                            99-045581

This book is dedicated to Lee Campbell, the mother of the birthparent movement. When she stepped out of the shadows of shame to declare her never-ending love for her son, she changed the nature of adoption forever.

Contents

Acknowledgments

Now and then, as I plugged away late in the evening trying to find words that were fresh and crunchy, it seemed that the writing of this book was a very solitary endeavor. With a bit of rest, though, that lonely impression would yield to the realization that this is anything but the project of an individual. The truth is, lots of people have contributed to this project, and they've done so in very significant ways. Some offered original ideas and insights, whereas others suggested improved ways to organize the material at hand. Some challenged sloppy formulations, while others offered timely encouragement. Some pointed out issues that I had overlooked; others urged sensible deletions. In concert, these diverse perspectives enriched this manuscript in countless ways. That so many friends would be so generous with their time leaves me dumbfounded.

At the risk of overlooking some folks—I suppose everybody I know has contributed in some manner or another—allow me to draw attention to a few whose assistance stood out. For starters, it was a pleasure to work again with CWLA editor Steve Boehm. Dutifully raising relevant questions, smoothing out rough spots, and even turning a phrase or two along the way, he did his job well. I can only wish for other writers that the editing process could be so painless.

I am thankful to Sharon Roszia, Randy Severson, Joyce Pavao, Bill Betzen, Marri Rillera, and Marcy Axness for reviewing the manuscript in its early stages. I am fortunate to count these open adoption stalwarts as friends. Their encouragement and suggestions helped me see the big picture and arrange my thoughts more clearly.

I am appreciative of Abbie Nelson and Doree Kent, my colleagues in the Values-Based Open Adoption Program at Catholic Human Services. They provide the close-at-hand discussion that is so valuable in feathering out the nuances of our practice. I continually find the respect they show for the people we serve a great inspiration. Thank goodness, too, for Dave Martin, the administrator at Catholic Human Services. Although it no doubt pains him at times, he has allowed me to operate as a bit of a maverick. I don't know what I would do if the system required that we make an assembly line out of our program.

Sometimes I think we are losing ground in the effort to normalize the institution of adoption, but other times I am encouraged by the emergence of new champions who speak boldly and lovingly for women and men dealing with awkward, untimely, or unsupported pregnancies. Professionals like Laurel Stitzhal from Open Adoption and Family Services in Seattle, Washington, and Renee Eifert from Catholic Social Services in Urbana, Illinois, come to mind as authentic champions for the birthparent cause. They offered useful commentary; but, better yet, it does me good to know they are out there making a difference.

I am most indebted to the many birthparents who have contributed to this project. Mirah Riben and Mary Anne Cohen offered constructive criticism that helped me avoid a dead end or two. Judi Larsen and her birthparent friends from Alberta provided valuable input as well. Among many others, Gail Cannon, Dawn Miner, Jennifer Huntsberry, Beverly Walker, and M.B. have had a great impact on my thinking. I appreciate the many helpful suggestions they made as they previewed this book. Even more importantly, I appreciate who they are. The word that comes to mind as I try to describe them is, get this, *wholesome*—not an adjective that birthparents hear routinely, I'm afraid, but a word that fits them well. Whenever I run into a situation where birthparents are being disparaged or written off, these folks come to mind. How can anyone think or say mean things about birthparents when people like these are numbered among them?

Two other birthparents deserve very special thanks. At different points in the process, Michelle Renaud and Heather Lowe went through the manuscript in astonishing detail. I cannot imagine how many hours they must have put into their responses. Their passion for the birthparent cause and for clear communication about this cause is so great that at times their suggestions filled all of the available space on the pages. Their contributions were gigantic, and I am deeply grateful.

Finally, I am thankful to all those birthparents who, through the years, allowed me to walk with them as they went through an amazing time in their lives. Your trust is an honor that I cannot get used to. You have blessed me beyond description with your examples of courage and costly love. I can only hope that this book in some small way returns the blessing.

Introduction

When our three daughters were little, there was nothing they enjoyed more than a rousing game of house. I happened to tune in to their proceedings one day and was intrigued by what I observed. A couple of close friends, Sara and Laura Vander Haagen—who happen to be open adoption kids— were on hand, and all five girls were consumed with serious negotiations about how the various household roles would be filled. Not surprisingly, the most cherished role was "Mom," and none of them were inclined to give up too easily on the chance to play this premier part in the drama.

I am sure similar rounds of hard-core dickering for the Mom position characterize games of house played around the world. The thing that fascinated me about this rendition was that the second role up for bid was "Birthmom," and I was impressed to see that they haggled over this position with nearly the same gusto. (Now, though, they had the benefit of a Mom to help them manage their wrangling!) The proceedings were lively and a joy to behold, although I must admit my pride was a little wounded to discover as the game moved forward that the bottom-of-the-barrel role for these young ladies was "Dad" and that part of the reason they worked so hard to land those earlier roles was to avoid a status so dreary.

The wonderful thing about this story is that it made sense to these children to hold the birthparent position in high regard. They didn't know about all the other ways birthparents are viewed; they just knew that birthparents can play an important part in the life of a family. As I see it, these young children knew something that many adults have not yet figured out.

1

Most of the time, birthparents are discounted. Whether young or more mature, scared or seemingly fearless, female or male, poor or financially comfortable, alone or surrounded with support, morally discredited or morally affirmed, birthparents are seldom allocated an influential or enduring place in the adoption process. Although they are obviously indispensable to the experience of adoption, they are mostly treated as though they are tangential to it. For a variety of reasons that we will explore in this book, birthparents are seldom full-status players in the drama of adoption.

Birthparents are marginalized in many ways. They are variously seen as bad, stupid, fickle, heartless, forgetful, dysfunctional, and disposable. We judge them, ignore them, pity them, "help" them, scorn them, fear them, use them, and put up with them. In an amazing number of ways, we create a safe and comfortable distance between "us" and "them." Sometimes, it seems the only version of birthparents we are unlikely to entertain is the idea that they might just be reasonably normal people like us.

No one seems quite sure what to make of birthparents. Who are they, anyway? Do they justly reap what they have sown, or are they victims of circumstances beyond their control? Are they morally suspect, or do they deserve our admiration? Can they really carry out and sustain the adoption decision, or will they eventually turn against it and seek to undo it? And what do we tell the children about them? If we paint birthparents as effective and strong, we raise a logical question as to why they decided to release their children for adoption. On the other hand, if we portray them as weak and unreliable, we fret about negative implications for the self-image of the children who are adopted. Anything but clear in its appraisal of birthparents, the adoption system is pleased when birthparents simply fade into the woodwork. With birthparents conveniently out of sight, we are spared the task of sorting through our contradictory thoughts about this befuddling collection of people. Everything seems so much simpler when the adoptive family system shrinks from the complexity of three major interactive parties to the relative simplicity of two.

For all of its neglect of birthparents, the system does find them at least briefly fascinating. As long as they hold the make-or-break power to decide whether there will be an adoption, potential birthparents are considered highly interesting and worthy of persistent and energetic courtship. Once the decision to move forward with adoption is legally made, however, and they have passed the point of no return, their stock routinely plummets. One moment everyone involved hangs on their every word; the next, it so often seems, no one really cares. As far as the system is concerned, the birthparent journey, for all practical purposes, ends at the point of legal relinquishment; it does not occur to very many people that birthparents are of long-term significance in the lifelong journey called adoption. The birthparent sun sets as swiftly as it rises.

We can do better than this. Our longstanding routine of looking the other way and hoping that birthparents will disappear is hardly the practice of adoption at its best. Birthparents are a conspicuously vulnerable group before, during, and after the tumultuous decision to entrust the everyday responsibilities of parenting to adoptive parents. They deserve far more than the system's embarrassing hope that they will evaporate. If we are serious about transforming adoption into a healthy institution, we must grow in our comprehension of who they are and what they go through. A good faith effort to more fully understand birthparents will benefit everyone involved with adoption. Most important, it will benefit the children they have brought to life.

I must admit to some trepidation about this project, for it is surely an anxious thing to write about a group that one is not a part of, most especially a collection of people whom I care about deeply. I write with good will, but there is a hazard that I understand too little of their reality to do justice to their cause. I must declare from the outset that I am an outsider to the birthparent experience. I am not a birthparent, nor am I female. All I can claim is that I am a social worker who has listened intently to hundreds of birthparents for more than two decades and that I have worked hard to make sense of what I have heard. Although I give great credence to the importance of insider accounts, I dare to hope that a keen listener has something important to offer. Perhaps I have some small advantage not being a birthparent, as this bit of distance may allow me a measure of objectivity that might not be available to me if I had lived out the experience. At any rate, I write in the hope that my observations will be of value to others who either are birthparents or who find them interesting.

Beyond listening, I am convinced there is another important way for those of us who are not birthparents to approach their experience. I am referring to imagination. I believe, if we take the time to imaginatively enter the experience of birthparents, each of us can find the "birthparent within" our own hearts. Deep thought informs me that I, for one, am capable of birthparenthood. When I let my imagination fully enter the situation, I can, in some circumstances, see myself making this decision. But I am not a happy birthparent. I do not yield easily. I go down with my fist to the sky, wondering how something so horrendous could be asked of me. I can feel the relentless, impersonal, nasty press of necessity, and I want to scream at the unfairness of it. I can feel the esteem-leveling beginnings of self-recrimination and loneliness. I am hyperalert—don't try to fool me—but I am also profoundly bewildered. Everything is out of control. For the first time in my life, I begin to wonder if my future is as promising as I always pictured it to be. I am indescribably hurt and suspicious. Prayer means more to me than ever before. I want somebody to try to understand me. I doubt they can, but I want them to try. My bones are sad. I am a bundle of worry. I want this crazy dream to stop.

For me, the dream does stop. For actual birthparents, obviously, it never ends.

Some readers will rightly wonder how birthfathers fit into the open adoption scene and why this book does not address them more specifically. Good questions. Part of the answer is that I have written about them before.* But there is more to it. It would be nice if birthfathers were routinely involved in these situations, but they are not. The first sentences in Susan Wadia-Ells's introduction to *The Adoption Reader* [1995] speak to this fact with great clarity.

> Adoption, like motherhood, has always been a woman's issue. It is women who give birth, and women who have had their birth children taken from them because of cultural, political or economic forces; and it is women who sometimes feel they must relinquish their birth child in order to protect that child [p. ix].

Anyone who is the least bit familiar with the adoption scene, who has attended an adoption conference, for example, quickly recognizes that it truly is feminine territory.

When it comes to birthfathers, we are caught uncomfortably between what the facts are and what we wish they were. We wish they were active participants on a regular basis, but too often they are not. For the sake of simplicity, then, this book yields to the frustrating reality of the largely absent birthfather and refers to birthparents with feminine

---

* James L. Gritter. (1997). *The Spirit of Open Adoption* (pp. 154–158). Washington D.C.: CWLA Press.

pronouns. Hopefully these pronouns will not obscure the fact that most of what is written applies equally to birthfathers. We must all do a better job of involving birthfathers, for their sake and for the benefit of their children.

For a while, in an effort to try to improve the image of birthparents who chose to entrust their child to a carefully selected family, I promoted the idea of distinguishing between voluntary and involuntary birthparents. I reasoned that it was a disservice to women who carefully and painstakingly arranged for another family to step into the caregiving role to be lumped together with parents who have lost the privilege of parenting as the result of neglect or abuse.

To my surprise, every birthparent I talked to hated the idea. I was trying to do them a favor, but the favor did not appeal to them for at least two reasons. First, they were not as certain as I was that their decision was all that voluntary—adoption was not, after all, something they were especially eager to do. "Voluntary," it turns out, was much too lighthearted for their taste. Second, to their great credit, they were in no hurry to besmirch the reputation of any other disadvantaged group. They had no interest in trying to improve their status by putting another group down. Without directly saying as much, they seemed to understand that highlighting the divisions between people is the problem, not the solution.

They are so correct. Now, instead of thinking in terms of volition, I talk about the challenge of working through "the necessity factor." Because necessity is a darker notion, it seems a more suitable way to approach the issue of birthparent motivation. And now, instead of trying to feather out differences between people, I do my best to point out how much we are alike.

I am convinced our approach to adoption must become more balanced. If we carry out a system that delights adoptive parents and works for most of the children but in the process destroys birthparents, where is the joy? Who can call that sort of outcome satisfactory? When will we learn that we are all in this together and that diminishing any one of us diminishes us all? We are never made larger by permitting others to be made smaller. The effort to elevate the status of birthparents need not in any way detract from the importance of adoptive parents. This is such a crucial observation that it is worth repeating: The effort to elevate the status of birthparents need not in any way detract from the importance of adoptive parents. Keeping birthparents involved in the lives of the children turns out to be good news for adoptive parents since it equips them to fill their roles more effectively and more joyfully than was previously possible. The only form of adoption that can be truly good news is one that acknowledges the interconnectedness of the participants and fully respects all of its members.

This book is an effort to explore various perceptions of birthparents and to grow in understanding of these intriguing folks. Within this inquiry, many issues are left unresolved. This will no doubt frustrate some readers who are eager to discover practical remedies for the issues they encounter. I understand their desire, but I sincerely doubt that the weighty themes of necessity, ambivalence, worthiness, grief, and regret that are woven through the birthparent experience will ever yield to simple formulas for relief. My intentions are more modest. I believe there is value in trying to understand the issues more clearly and in gaining greater perspective. My hope is that, as we grow in understanding of birthparents, we will fear them less and respect them more. Perhaps we can grow to the point where we see ourselves mirrored in their struggles and fully identify with them. Fate, after all, could have made birthparents out of many of us. If we think for a moment that birthparents are different from the rest of us, we deceive ourselves.

Surely the most formidable impediment to a healthier perspective on birthparents is fear. Because so little is known about birthparents, they inspire fear. That observation will no doubt strike some birthparents as hilarious—so much of the time they feel so puny and powerless—but it is true. They are feared because they are unknown and mysterious. They are feared because they are thought to be unusual. And they are feared because they are tragic, sorrowful figures.

Because we have so much power to wound each other in our relationships, some fear is inevitable in open adoption, but we do not have to fear their ambivalence and sadness. When we come to see ambivalence and sadness as normal expressions of the undying love birthparents have for their children, we begin to make room for them in our hearts. When we learn to respect and embrace these lifegivers for their courage rather than driving them from the pack as outcasts, I believe everyone involved will be better off. As we come to see birthparents as constructive, ongoing players in the adoption drama, we can move forward with a warmer and more wholesome version of adoption than we ever imagined.

If children can figure it out, so can the rest of us.

Part 1

Limiting Perceptions

Chapter 1

Why the Public Dislikes Birthparents (And Why They Are Wrong)

Okay, maybe *dislike* is too strong a word, but does anyone want to step forward and make the case that the public is particularly fond of birthparents? I didn't think so.*

An odd thing, isn't it, this disaffection for birthparents? Young, earthy, vulnerable, lifegiving, and abortion-transcending, one might suppose that birthparents would routinely capture the public's imagination and affection, but they seldom do. If anything, the standard reaction to birthparents is a raised eyebrow and a dismissive "tsk tsk"— much as it was decades ago. Birthparents, it seems, are to be endured, not endeared. Why is this? Why do they gather so little public appreciation?

Part of the trouble is that most people know birthparents but aren't aware that they do. We know them in other capacities—teachers and nurses, aunts and cousins, neighbors and friends—but seldom do we know about their life-altering connection to adoption. For reasons of grief, shame, and reasonable privacy, most birthparents keep a very low profile. So low is their profile that even those who are close to them are often unaware of their experience.

---

* Interestingly, several birthmothers who previewed the manuscript for this book commented that *dislike* is much too weak a word for what they encounter. They feel hated.

Amazing though it seems, some birthparents will not even permit themselves to acknowledge that they are birthparents. They do not think of themselves as birthparents; it isn't something they allow into their consciousness, and it certainly isn't part of their public identity. They have seen the cool disdain other birthparents have weathered, and they presume a similar fate awaits them if their stories become known. A few birthparents, of course, become notorious for various reasons, but most keep their heads down and do their best to avoid attention.

Understandable as it is, the invisibility of "average" birthparents adds to the unfortunate likelihood that, as a group, they will be misunderstood. In the absence of knowable people, we usually turn to popular images and stereotypes of birthparents. What are these images that create our impressions of birthparents, and where do these images come from?

Common Images of Birthparents

Public opinion about birthparents does not appear to have much foundation. When people are pressed to identify the origins of their impressions, answers are invariably vague. People largely form their opinions from things they have read somewhere or things they have heard. Some recall, "I sort of knew a girl back in high school who...." Others say they have learned about birthparents from television, leaving open the question whether it was from purported news shows or soap operas. These dubious sources of information provide a variety of stereotypes, most of which are both inaccurate and unflattering.

The Fallen Woman. Perhaps the most prominent and lasting image of birthparents is that of "the fallen woman," whose wardrobe features a scarlet letter. Failing to meet social standards, she absorbs her community's disapproval and contempt through every pore. Her fallen status severely diminishes her standing and her sense of worthiness. Even the more benevolent image of the "good girl who got caught" is mostly negative since whatever virtue the young woman may possess is easily outweighed by her foolishness in getting caught. Although we no longer literally speak of the fallen woman, the stereotype of the wild-living, disreputable, promiscuous party girl persists. In comparison with such recklessness, most people feel smug and superior.

The Ineffectual Woman. Community disapproval is gradually shifting from indignation over wayward behavior to suspicion of a general ineffectiveness. These days she is viewed not so much as a moral failure but as a failure in practical terms who has somehow brought her problems upon herself. Why wasn't she smart enough to protect herself from pregnancy? Why didn't she discretely "take care" of this awkward situation? Why can't she get herself together so she can raise her baby herself? In the view of budget-tightening social critics, she has made a mess of things, and there is little sympathy for her plight. They wonder with irritation, "Why can't she be responsible and keep things under control like the rest of us?"

The Fickle Woman. The birthparent is often viewed as a capricious mind changer, a notion the media has inflated with its sensational coverage of a handful of contested custody cases. In the eyes of many, she is a threat to the deserving prospective adoptive parents, the parties in the adoption drama with whom the public identifies most easily because they are solidly middle class, morally upright, and long-suffering victims of heartbreaking infertility. Even in problem-free circumstances, the public wonders if the birthmother has seriously underestimated the primal appeal of parenting and worries that eventually she will change her mind about the adoption and make trouble. The birthmother is much more likely to be seen as a threat to the stability of adoption than as the courageous person who makes it possible in the first place.

The Denigrated Woman. As if she didn't have enough trouble on her own, the birthparent is associated with a variety of low-status characters. For starters, even if she has chosen to entrust her child to an adoptive family for the best of reasons, her role is associated with parents whose rights have been terminated because of abuse and neglect. By that association, she is under suspicion as someone who might mistreat children if given the chance. She is also eyed as a prospective welfare recipient, cut from the same sullied cloth as those villainous drainers of civic resources that so annoy the public. She is numbered among the underclass of the powerless and unimportant—young, poor, and female. Perceived as desperate, unpredictable, and having little to lose, the disadvantaged person has a way of making the comfortable uncomfortable.

The Tormented Woman. The birthparent's image loses additional luster when linked to some deeply unhappy and occasionally strident voices from the previous generation of birthparents. These victims of a punitive system of adoption have much to teach, but the angry tone of their commentary— though it is often merited—rouses a defensive reaction and works against their purposes.

When it comes to adoption, most people seem quite willing to put their heads in the sand. The public wholeheartedly supports adoption and, in an era of eroding consensus, views it as one of the last happy stories on which everyone can agree. The positive mythology of adoption appeals to the public because adoption is seen as a promising alternative for the burgeoning number of children who are stuck in the system. Adoption is an icon of societal generosity and hope, and our communities are prepared, if necessary, to consider it with a blind eye.

Given this cheery view of adoption, it is no surprise that the public instinct is to defend it. So, instead of judging the circumstances that stir the anger of past birthparents, the public reacts impatiently and unhappily to those curmudgeons who have the audacity to challenge the myth. The public swiftly dismisses these critics because their message does not feel constructive. Because her anguish ruins a happy story, most people wish the birthparent would just be quiet.

The Heartless Woman. Although seldom made explicit, the most damaging perception of the birthparent is that she is violating a vital, nonnegotiable societal expectation. Few of us understand or appreciate the idea of a mother setting aside her maternal role, because we fully expect mothers to stick with their children no matter what. It is a cultural norm inculcated so deeply that it makes sense in our bones. We enjoy timeless humor that "only a mother could love a kid who...."

This deep-seated belief in the inviolable mother-child bond causes more uneasiness among adoption observers than any other factor. Because of the belief that mothers ought to "hang in there come what may," the adoption decision strikes many onlookers as unnatural, and it unnerves them in ways most cannot fully understand or articulate. It simply goes against the grain. Giving voice to this line of thought, some critics characterize the adoption decision as an act of irresponsibility and insinuate it is the "easy way out" of a challenging circumstance. This is a dumbfounding and maddening accusation for birthparents who uniformly describe the entrusting of a child to adoptive parents as the most difficult decision they have ever encountered.

If the public has a hard time appreciating birthmothers, it finds birthfathers almost impossible to like. In the eyes of many, birthfathers are threats to the prospect of adoption with few if any redeeming qualities. They are presumed guilty of many sins: casually impregnating innocent women, failing to provide necessary financial and emotional support, pressuring their partners into unlikable decisions, and cavalierly thwarting adoption intentions. Most people have very little information about birthfathers—they are even more invisible than birthmothers—but seem to know enough to reach the conclusion that they do not like them.

The Impact of an Unfavorable Birthparent Image

The negative image of birthparents is not simply a pesky, unfortunate matter; it has consequences that profoundly affect the nature of the adoption experience. Their minimal status adds to their vulnerability and places them at serious risk for exploitation by more powerful players in the drama. Marginalized by mystery and misunderstanding, birthparents become "them," a dubious group set apart. Since they are different from "us," public opinion is wary at best. In stronger terms, they are feared. The public holds birthparents at arm's length and treats them as guilty until they prove their innocence. As Timothy Uhlmann, a colleague from the earliest days of open adoption practice at our agency, Catholic Human Services, bluntly recalls, "Birthparents were treated as quasi-criminals without any franchise in the decision-making process." Chronically under suspicion, birthparents are clearly less than full prestige players in the adoption drama, and the system feels justified in paying little heed to their interests.

In some ways, the institution seems to prefer or perhaps even requires a negative perception of birthparents. An unfavorable view of birthparents makes the system sensible and morally tidy. If birthparents are disreputable, children are no doubt advantaged to be liberated from their dubious influence, and the entire institution seems neatly justified. On the other hand, if birthparents were well-regarded, adoption would not be quite so conspicuously wonderful. As birthparent and adoption educator Brenda Romanchik points out, the public has a heartier appetite for good-guy-versus-bad-guy stories than it does for moral ambiguity.

Sadly, the negative image of birthparents affects their prospects within an open adoption relationship. Operating with diminished moral standing, few birthparents enter these relationships surefooted. On what basis, then, do they participate?

A few, very few, are bold enough to kick the door down. Assertive by nature and practice, they demand a continuing role in the lives of their children. They are not worried about being liked or appreciated. They know they have some raw power, at least early on, and they are not reluctant to use it to accomplish their purposes on behalf of their sons and daughters. They are players to contend with, whether others like it or not. Some people understand and admire their resolve, but more often their assertiveness is resented.

More commonly, birthparents are "permitted" to play a part in their adoptions. On this basis, the system maintains control and good-naturedly doles out carefully measured opportunities for participation. Although this approach often works reasonably well, the crucial point for birthparents is that they remain dependent on the charity of others, a far less pleasing status than inclusion because one naturally belongs. In some ways, accepting a continuing role based on the system's "generosity" is to concede the assumption that birthparents rightly operate with reduced worthiness. If birthparents were held in higher regard, they would be involved because of their conspicuous importance to their children and out of recognition of their intrinsic value as persons, not because of the compassion of others.

Fortunately, many birthparents establish genuine friendships with the adoptive families that transcend the original wariness of the arrangement. As healthy interaction between the families moves forward, warmth and trust grow in natural fashion. In the best of circumstances, birthparents are involved because they are fully respected and because everyone knows they belong. They do not just have a point-in-time contribution to make but are recognized as participants with enduring importance. On this basis of respect, they are full-status members of the open adoption community.

In addition to diminishing their prospects for meaningful ongoing involvement with their children, the dismal image of birthparents affects the other parties involved in adoption. Adoptive parents are often perplexed as they try to understand the nature of their relationship with their child's birthparents. Is the relationship, they wonder, that of peers, or are they supposed to somehow benevolently reach out to birthparents and help them? The perceived low standing of birthparents may tempt adoptive parents subtly or not so subtly to claim the moral high ground. "Aren't we swell for being so considerate?" If that happens, interaction between the families will have a dispiriting feel of patronage. On those terms, the connection between the families is more likely to maim the participants than heal them.

The discounted status of birthparents carries great meaning for adopted children, meaning that can be played out in many forms. Negative stereotypes of birthparents can undermine the children's self-image. The children may infer they are from substandard origins and function accordingly. If their birthparents are suspicious characters, they reason, maybe they are genetically destined to replicate their birthparents' shortcomings. Maybe they, too, are fated to fall short of societal expectations.

A Closer Look at Birthparents

We have seen that the image of birthparents is unappealing. Does reality match the image? In some ways, it doesn't matter. Even if birthparents were the derelicts that the stereotypes make them out to be, they would, nevertheless, as human beings deserve reasonable and respectful treatment. A closer look, though, reveals that the typical birthparent who chooses to entrust her child to adoptive parents is very different from the prevailing image. Anyone who makes the effort to get to know birthparents will quickly discover many remarkable people with very impressive value systems. The ironic observation that they may hold higher moral standards than many of their critics makes it easier to afford them a full measure of respect and standing.

Pregnancy at an inopportune time in life raises complex moral questions. I believe we learn at least as much about the moral strength of these folks from the way they work through their situations as we do from the circumstances leading to their pregnancies. The adoption choice reveals a great deal about their character and basic values. Let's take a closer look at some of the beliefs commonly held by people who consider adoption as a possible life course for their children. While not everyone will agree with the reasoning that goes into their beliefs, most will at least concede that their intentions are honorable.

- Birthparents believe children benefit from early life stability. Although many people hold that babies are endlessly adaptable, mothers who choose adoption for their children have a different perspective. They are convinced that children benefit from consistency and believe that adoption—even with its worrisome early transition from one family to another—is the course that offers the greatest consistency. They also see how readily economic hardship can replace steadiness and security with chaos and hazard. They want to do everything they can to maximize their children's life chances and are unwilling to settle for marginal circumstances.

- Birthparents believe in the importance of fathers. In contemporary times, this belief sets them apart. We have become so accustomed to single parenting that we have allowed the importance of fathers to be belittled; we have sometimes acted as though they are optional or expendable. In contrast to societal nonchalance about fathers, birthparents believe they play vital, indispensable roles in the lives of children.

- Open adoption birthparents believe their children deserve a full accounting as to how the adoption decision was made. They also believe that their children deserve ongoing respect, love, and encouragement from their families of origin. Although they entrust the daily care of their children to carefully selected parents, they continue to stand by their children, even at times that may not be especially convenient.

- Birthparents are realistic and forward-looking. Everyone loves to fuss over babies, but not everyone has the patience and energy to deal with the toddlers and teenagers they become. In many instances, birthparents have an unusually keen sense of the realities that lie ahead coupled with rare honesty about their ability to follow through and unresentfully meet the formidable challenges associated with parental responsibility.

- Birthparents are able to set aside their personal preferences for the benefit of their children. Adoption is never an easy choice for birthparents; it is always a matter of sorrowful necessity. Believing that adoption is genuinely the most promising path for their children, they choose it even though it causes them indescribable loss and emptiness. The elevation of the children's needs over their own is an amazing act of love.

- Birthparents are doggedly independent and are reluctant to draw on the support of others. Their belief in rugged individualism—the quintessential American value—is fierce and costly; if they were willing to set aside this conviction and accept public assistance, they might be able to retain custody of their children.

- Birthparents value themselves and act with appropriate self-interest. Although they recognize their children's importance and make sacrifices for them, they also attend to their own reasonable needs. They are, after all, someone's child, too. The adoption decision is very costly to them emotionally, but for many it also holds important personal advantages.

- Birthparents have the strength of character to carry through their beliefs. The reality of pregnancy powerfully tests opinions about pregnancy outcomes formed in comfortable abstraction. It is not unheard of for people to set aside prior beliefs in the face of the wilting pressure of an untimely, awkward, or unsupported pregnancy. Whatever our position on abortion, we do well to appreciate that many birthparents courageously translate their beliefs into action. Conviction causes them to tread the road less traveled.

Not all birthparents, of course, act with so much conviction. Birthparents present a full cross section of humanity, and their ranks range from saints to scalawags. Few are saints, and few are scalawags; mostly they are just average people. Some are less admirable than others, but, as flesh and blood creatures doing the best they can in extremely anxious circumstances, they all deserve fair-minded consideration.

Moving Toward Acceptance and Respect

The negative image of birthparents is destructive and unwarranted—it calls out for correction. To ignore this dynamic is to allow its perpetuation. The scurrilous mythology of birthparenthood is deeply entrenched, so a formidable effort is necessary to correct it. Those who join forces to address the issue have their hands full. There will be resistance. We know in advance that some people, concrete-thinking holders of the taboo, for example, will never understand the message, but we cannot be deterred by the difficulty of the task. I believe four things must happen if the image of birthparents is to improve.

First, we need birthparents to step forward and publicly share their experiences. Happily, in this era of open adoption, this is beginning to happen with greater frequency. It is not yet common, however. Healthy spokespersons of the present generation of birthparents are usually well received, but too often they are written off as exceptions because there are so few of them. Hopefully, this offhand dismissal will happen less often as the public gets to know more of them.

This stepping forward is no small thing. Given the societal mind-set regarding adoption and birthparents, it is hardly surprising that birthparents feel incredibly exposed and vulnerable when they tell their stories. It takes courage for them to speak out. While they seldom face frontal assaults by critics and naysayers, they can expect to be wounded by thoughtless and blundering comments from underinformed respondents, both friend and foe.

As more hearty souls muster the chutzpah to share their stories, however, we will begin to replace debilitating stereotypes with bona fide people with whom the public can relate and identify. When this happens, general confidence in their fundamental humanness will grow. No one, obviously, can represent the world of birthparents better than they can themselves, and no evidence of their decency could be more convincing than their own sincere testimony and simple presence as loving and lovable persons.

Second, the adoptive community must rise to defend the honor of birthparents. Everyone in a position to know birthparents—social workers, clergy, judges, friends, and extended family—must support the honor of birthparents. This is especially true of adoptive parents who are too often cast as adversaries. Adoption ought never be organized as a proprietary tussle between birthparents and adoptive parents. Rather, it is better understood as an exercise in cooperation. We must all vouch for the decency of birthparents and actively confront and correct the stereotypes that thoughtlessly roll off so many tongues. We must not allow people we encounter to speak lightly of birthparents in disparaging terms and carry on in the exasperating tone of voice that suggests "everyone knows" they are a worrisome lot. Beyond the correcting of stereotypes, we can, as members of the broader community, proactively speak of our admiration for the courage of birthparents. Like the rest of us, they have flaws, but their gutsy love for their children should never be overlooked.

Third, the wider adoptive community must do a better job of identifying with birthparents. Hopefully, we can soften our quick-to-judge hearts and relate to the tragic dimensions of their circumstances. As we honestly face our own shortcomings, we will likely grow in our ability to identify with theirs. Instead of distancing ourselves by accentuating differences, we can emphasize our common nature. If we take the time to fire our imaginations and discover the "birthparent within" each of us, the presumed gap between us vanishes instantly. Once we recognize that we, too, in the grip of a desperate situation are capable of this sorrowful decision, we are positioned to understand and embrace their anguish.

Finally, we must develop a new script for the appropriate transfer of parental responsibility. As the open adoption process becomes more familiar and the significance of lifegivers is more fully delineated, there is reasonable hope that the strength and character of birthparents will become more obvious and that their choice of adoption will be understood as a mature act of love. We need to question the taboo against a mother's separation from her children so that exceptions are allowed when they are in the best interests of children. A societal attitude that permits and even endorses the thoughtful transfer of parental rights in circumstances of great necessity would do much to counter and relieve the public's concern about the violation of the maternal taboo.

This is all part of a paradigm shift. The closed system assumed birthparent shame. That system justified the movement of a child from one family to another explicitly as a matter of socioeconomic opportunity and implicitly as a matter of moral progress. Open adoption does not need a finding of unworthiness in one party and worthiness in the other; it functions best on the premise that adoptive parents and birthparents draw equally from the same wonderful yet flawed well of human nature. Having overcome fear and skepticism with a spirit of mutuality and cooperation, each participant stands fully worthy of our respect.

This dramatic shift in the public's perspective will take time and effort. If we do somehow jettison our prejudices and come to view birthparents positively, we can expect the face of adoption to change dramatically. Instead of teetering uncomfortably on the edge of an exploitative dynamic in which the "worthy" benefit at the expense of the "unworthy," adoption will shine with the decency of reciprocal affirmation. We will not, however, enjoy a health-generating ethic of honor in adoption until we learn to view birthparents as fully deserving of our respect.

And who knows? If we make the effort to know birthparents, we might just discover that they are a pretty likable bunch.

Chapter 2

"What Kind of Woman...?" Taboo Breaking and the Pursuit of Worthiness

One question, phrased a thousand ways, hounds all birthmothers: "What kind of woman could give her baby away?" It is the scourge of birthmothers everywhere. When this query is placed at the doorstep of a particular individual, it is often stated in point blank terms: "How could you do such a thing?" Occasionally this is a genuine question, a sincere pursuit of information, but most of the time it's more accusation than inquiry. Seldom is it followed with an expectant pause that awaits explanation because, presumably, no answer could possibly satisfy the inquiry. The "question" is routinely punctuated with a dismissive shrug of the shoulders. The shrug is definitive and declares the obvious: Anyone and everyone knows that mothers and children are meant to stay together—it's a no-brainer. We may hold a mixture of feelings about mothers, but we never doubt their loyalty. This primal relationship is like no other. When it comes to the connection between mothers and children, there are no options; they are stuck with each other for life whether they like it or not. It's just the way it is. Maternity is not erasable.

Interestingly, this accusing question hardly ever takes the compassionate form that wonders, "What were the circumstances that required this mother to make such a painful decision?" When a taboo is in question, our instinct is to judge the person rather than the circumstance. When the unthinkable happens, we want to know what kind of person would do such a thing. In this manner, taboo breaking has less to do with guilt than with shame. It is less concerned with unacceptable behavior than with the unacceptable people who behave in unconventional fashion. This emphasis on character rather than behavior explains the great shaping power of taboos. One might risk an occasional unacceptable act, but one does not lightly risk becoming an unacceptable person.

So, what kind of woman makes such a decision? For taboo enforcers, the answer is swift and certain. A heartless woman, someone who flat out does not give a rip, that's who. As they see it, this is the only possible answer, and any effort to explain or defend her decision is a waste of time. Parting ways with a child is an unnatural act, and anyone who does something so unthinkable is obviously a different kind of person. And let's be clear, this is not a happy version of different. No doubt about it, "a woman like that" who goes against the timeless internalized wisdom of both nature and community has significantly less merit than other, more conventional citizens.

Those who hold the taboo most intensely are usually very concrete thinkers who see things in black-and-white terms. Confident they hold the moral high ground, they make short work of the subject. In many instances, these critics are less sophisticated than the targets of their moral analysis, and their matter-of-fact, unreflective criticism galls and appalls the birthparent who has poured around-the-clock, conscience-probing thought into her decision. Often there is little she can do to defend herself against these esteem-leveling verdicts because she and the accuser speak very different languages. Although her circumstances typically have very tangible aspects—like being financially broke—the birthparent's cause must largely be pled in abstract terms. These abstractions are nonsense to the taboo holder. Ironically, while the concrete-thinking critic may also be opposed to abortion, early marriage, and single parenting—leaving no acceptable means of handling the situation—he or she is probably enthusiastic about the idea of worthy people adopting children. According to this logic, it's all right for people to adopt children, it's just not okay for parents to allow their children to be adopted.

Abstract thinkers and concrete thinkers find it painfully difficult to understand each other. This truth stood out in an animated conversation to which I was privy between an expectant mother and father who found themselves pregnant quite by surprise. Not only did this couple obviously love each other, they also clearly needed each other. He had exceptional physical strength, whereas she was weak because of an accident. She was unusually sensitive and bright, while he struggled with various learning disabilities. He was fond of saying, "I am her legs, and she is my brain. Together we are strong."

Blunt by nature, he was not much given to subtlety of thought. When she expressed interest in exploring the possibility of adoption, he responded with a tirade of contempt: "WHAT? ADOPTION? How could you say such a thing? What is wrong with you? Don't you have any kind of heart? All this time I thought you were a nice person, and now look what you're talking about! Don't you like babies? Are you so heartless you would turn your back on your own baby? Don't you care? Don't you feel any responsibility? What kind of person are you? What kind of woman are you? I've never heard anything so selfish! Is there no love in your heart at all? I never thought you could be so rotten. Who would have thought you could look so sweet and be so cruel! I'm appalled. You make me sick."

As he lambasted the prospect of adoption at great length and with unrestrained vigor, it never occurred to him that he was commenting on his beloved's character or that she might take his comments personally. Not surprisingly, her words about "greater stability" or "more opportunity" did not carry much weight in his league.

The searing intimation that birthparents are cut from different cloth usually takes much subtler form. Some of this thinking is even meant to be supportive. Adoptive parents, for example, frequently comment, "I'm impressed. I could never be so unselfish." Or peers comment lightly, "You did what was right. That's exactly what I would have done." Unfortunately, their tone of voice makes it clear that they have little idea of the anguish that went into the decision. Comments like these are well intended, but they supply little comfort to birthparents whose perceptions are keenly tuned to statements carrying valuative content. Each comment unwittingly invokes the taboo. Each remark is a small but powerful reminder of difference, of the fact that birthmothers have strayed from the standard course of maternal behavior. The observations are meant to salute the emotional strength of the birthparent, but instead they push an emotional button that tells her she is different from and less than others. What was meant as "Well done" often stirs the uncomfortable thought, "Oh, so you're better than me, eh?"

The accusing query grates on birthparents' nerves whenever it comes up and whatever form it takes. It irritates when a completely uninformed person raises it inadvertently, but it hurts most when it comes from people in a position to know better. Family and friends offend more often through little lapses than in direct assaults. "Do you know what you're doing?" they ask as the monumental point of decision approaches, implying rather transparently that they have their doubts. As insiders, they know the heart of the birthmother, and they are also well acquainted with the gravity of her circumstance. Being close to the action, however, does not necessarily mean they understand what is going on. I recall one mother of a struggling birthmother declaring, "I said I would support you in any decision you made, but I had hoped, of course, you wouldn't make this one." Hmm, they call this support?

Sometimes these close associates are just not thinking. Supposing that custody defines motherhood, they might, for example, overlook the importance of Mother's Day for the birthmother. Sometimes they are embarrassed by their taboo-breaking relative and do their best to downplay her adoption story. Birthparenting is not something they are pleased to see on their loved one's résumé, and they may occasionally concoct an awkward explanation to avoid telling someone the truth of the matter. The discomfort that underlies the fumbling evasion is not lost on the birthparent, for it suggests to her that she is an embarrassment to her family.

By far, the most dreaded version of "How could you?" looms in the questioning eyes of the child. Every birthmother I have met has worried at one time or another that her child "will grow up to hate me." This "how could you" is formidable; it tests one's character. The adoptee is, of course, interested in the circumstances that necessitated the adoption decision, but mostly he wants to peer into his birthmother's heart. What, really, he wonders, was this all about? A question from his soul deserves an answer from hers, and she prays she can somehow find ways to explain her lonely experience, all the while knowing this is an experience for which there is no adequate language.

Disapproval for the decision to entrust a child to the care of others is common, but it is not universal. Thankfully, many people are able to identify with the difficulty of the birthparent circumstance and reflexively respond with care and respect.

They do not see birthparents as taboo breakers or lesser beings; they see them as strong but hurting persons who stand in need of understanding. Their respectful interest is very healing for birthparents who long for signals of acceptance. Their sincerity makes a difference.

I remember a friendly hallway conversation with an adoptive mother during a conference break. After she shared a "they're better than me, I could never do that" comment, I pointed out that birthparents often take that sort of remark as a put down. With a determined edge to her voice she responded, "Well, I really mean it. I've thought about this a lot, and I'm convinced that the birthmother of our son is a stronger person than I am. She did what she knew was right, and that took great courage. The truth is, there are plenty of times when I do not follow through on what I know to be right. She really is a stronger person than I am, and I can't even begin to tell you how much I admire her." The determined look in her face made it clear that she was prepared to take the discussion further if need be.

This adoptive mother believes in birthparents, and she means business. With her conviction and her willingness to speak up, she makes the world a better place for birthparents. The good news is that she is not alone. As more and more people come to know birthparents as a result of the open approach to adoption, allies are gained every day.

Can Separation Really Be an Expression of Love?

There are growing pockets of understanding, yet much work remains to be done. Part of the problem is that most people settle for a superficial understanding of adoption. They are so caught up in the excitement of seeing a family expand that they overlook the anguish of the family that loses one of its

own. This loss is routinely underestimated. Pregnant women are enthusiastically reassured that "adoption is a loving
choice," but, in the ears of many, the rhetoric often rings
hollow. The platitude that was meant to reassure instead feels
unauthentic and cosmetic. The attempt to "pretty up" the loss
and sadness of adoption strikes many as unconvincing. Often
this cheerful chatter feels like propaganda from folks with an
agenda that is not especially tuned to the needs and realities
of particular individuals.

If the case is to be convincingly made that open adoption
can be a loving choice, it cannot feature a cushy form of love
that rolls off the tongue in glib, sentimental tones. I doubt
glossy brochures with smiling Gerber babies and reassuring
words about love convince very many pregnant women that
adoption is a great and tender idea. To the contrary, these
appealing images may prompt her to think, "Who could resist
such a beautiful child? What's wrong with me that I am not
planning to be a mother?" Her own voice joins with so many
others in speculation about the kind of woman who chooses
not to take on the maternal role.

Don't get me wrong. I do believe adoption can be a loving
choice, but I am convinced this kind of love is not soft and
cute. It's an awful form of love, a tough, tearful, costly version of love that rattles a person's core. It has a lot more to do
with midnight pacing and tear-smirched journals than with
frilly affectations. This is the sort of devastating love that
redefines a person's life story, and it deserves far more than
candy coating.

Does it ever make sense to say, "I love you so much that I
must step away from you?" The idea seems odd to us because
we usually see love as a force that brings people together.
We are far more accustomed to hearing, "I love you so much
that I want to be with you forever." Separation does not
ordinarily come to mind when we speak of love, yet this line

of action is not entirely foreign to us. In fact, nearly all parents know something about it. As a brave-of-face-but-sad-in-heart parent who has deposited a brave-of-face-but- sad-in-heart daughter in a sterile college dorm where she did not know anybody, I know something about this subject. That much anticipated, awkward moment was a bittersweet echo of the day many years earlier when we watched our intrepid firstborn joyfully pile into a waiting school bus.

Admittedly, the loss I am describing is minuscule compared to the loss experienced by birthparents, but it does demonstrate that there are times when the loving course of action is to step back so the loved one can step forward. I also know there is more of the same awaiting me. Someday, a walking jumble of joy and melancholy, I will accompany my daughter down the church aisle in another journey of loving separation. We have mixed feeling about it, but parental love regularly calls us to back off and let go. In doing this, we do not abandon our children; we entrust them to themselves and others who love them so they can grow as persons.

So, after painstaking thought, we recognize the stepping back of birthparents as love. We must be careful in this discussion, though, of going too far with this line of thought. Too much talk of heroic, sacrificial love makes birthparents uneasy. Most birthparents I know do not like being nominated for sainthood any more than they like being written off as uncaring persons. They know neither version is true. They simply hope for acceptance as normal people struggling to do the best they can in extremely difficult circumstances.

Self-Worth and Low Self-Esteem

To the extent they feel abandoned by others or even banished from the pack, birthparents find it difficult to feel good about themselves. For all of the contemporary bravado urging us to disregard the opinions others may have about us, none of us can escape the pervasive impact of our social context. Like it or not, we take many cues about our identity and worth from the people around us. In many ways, we are what we see in the eyes of our neighbors. When birthparents look into the eyes of their neighbors, they often perceive disapproval. Perhaps without a word being said—the faint twitch of an eyebrow is more than sufficient—birthparents are reminded that they have not measured up to expectations, and they feel shamefully defective.

The real power of community criticism, of course, is that it confirms impressions that have already occurred to birthparents. It's amazing how willing we are as humans to accept the conclusion that we have fallen short and are failures. The adoption decision may leave a birthparent with a feeling that acts as a devastating inversion of guilt. In a circumstance of guilt, a good person feels bad that she did something wrong. Reflecting on her decision in the context of community disapproval, a birthparent may reach the extraordinary conclusion that she is a bad person because she did the right thing—a confusing state of being that wears her down. Emotionally exhausted from her ordeal, and struggling with misgivings about her acceptability as a person, she is inclined to accept her cast-off status. This capitulation to self-doubt is very consequential, for the world feels like a very different place when one has lost one's sense of being acceptable.

Feelings of unworthiness are often strongest for the most capable birthparent. The greater the respect and prominence she held in her community before her untimely pregnancy and subsequent adoption decision, the more she feels she has let everybody down, herself included. I'm reminded of a young lady for whom I helped arrange an outstanding open adoption several years ago. Bright, attractive, athletic, and gifted in the theater arts, "Sally" was a high school superstar.

Slated to attend an elite university, she looked forward to an unlimited future. When she became pregnant unexpectedly in her senior year, all of her plans were suddenly in jeopardy. Unsure what to do and under not so subtle pressure from her family, she reluctantly conceded that the best way to handle her situation was to arrange for her child to be adopted. The idea was that adoption would allow her to pursue her dreams of advanced education and ultimately a professional career.

Things didn't exactly work according to plan. When I ran into her most recently, she was working as a clerk at a department store. She told me that she had dropped out of college after a couple of years. She had "never been able to find" herself in the years since the adoption was arranged and had spent her time "drifting" from relationship to relationship. As Sally shared her story, it occurred to me that the worthiness issues raised by her adoption decision were far more powerful than anyone had anticipated. Instead of permitting her to move ahead toward greater effectiveness, adoption had instead become a gateway to ineffectiveness.

There is no way to adequately describe the impact of lost personal worth because it flavors everything in the birthmother's existence. Sadly, the feeling of unworthiness cancels many possibilities as she backs off from a variety of opportunities. Over and over, she tells herself she is "not cut out for" constructive activities, that she is "not suited for" exciting possibilities that pop up, or that she "doesn't deserve" respectful treatment. With these thoughts running through her mind, her world steadily shrinks, and her isolation grows.

Low self-esteem manifests itself in so many ways that space permits the mention of only a few of the forms it may take. It commonly takes a toll on the birthmother's relationships. Having reached the jarring conclusion that she was not the person best suited to raise her child, she concludes that she is not worthy to participate in any major relationship. Significantly, the feeling of unworthiness may undercut her confidence to visit the adoptive family. Uncomfortable in the presence of "good" people like the "worthy" adoptive parents, she may seek the company of dubious characters who are quite willing to treat her in the shabby fashion she believes she deserves. Some birthmothers predict rejection and launch preemptive strikes of unworthiness, as if to say, "Let me tell you how awful I am before you discover this on your own."

One especially sad conclusion she may reach is to doubt that she deserves to have additional children. If she was not adequate to meet the needs of one child, she wonders, how could she be adequate for another? Instead of linking the decision to the pressing circumstances of that particular moment in time, she attaches the decision to her sense of unworthiness. The prospect of having another child stirs a corollary of the taboo—mothers are expected to treat their children equally. How could she entrust one child to an adoptive family and raise another herself? How does she explain this to her children?

Coming to Terms with the Taboo

Relief from the cloud of societal judgment and self-judgment can be gained in various ways, but it's not likely to be found by arguing with the fundamental validity of the taboo. Some will no doubt press forward with the argument that the taboo is invalid, but I believe, because taboos are by nature close to immutable, they will not get far.

Actually, for the most part, birthparents agree with the taboo. Birthmothers have no quarrel with the idea that mothers and children are important to each other and that it is best when they can stay together. The power of the taboo, in fact, helps them make the point that it is desirable for them to stay in contact with their children. This respect for the essence of the taboo opens some common ground for discussion with those who enforce it. It enlivens the hope that it may be possible to persuade our communities to think about the mother-child bond more carefully. Perhaps the public can come to see that its thinking in this matter needs some refining. In its present form, the taboo is a clumsy, heavy-handed form of social control that sometimes produces outcomes that are counter to its purpose. Its function, after all, is to ensure that children are effectively nurtured, but this intention is not always best served by insisting that mothers stay on duty in every circumstance. Clearly, alternate care sometimes offers a child a better chance to thrive.

The argument, then, is not with the intent of the taboo but with its rigid application. Clearly, we must make allowances for reasonable exceptions, although there may be room for discussion regarding the circumstances leading to them. The imperative that requires mothers and children to stay together remains valid, but we need an acceptable script for the responsible transfer of maternal authority from one mother to another in some instances. If we can establish this exception, then birthparents who fall within its parameters could be spared censure for taking the course they believe to be most responsible.

Recovering Self-Worth

There are many ways for a birthparent to regain her sense of self-worth. Some have little to do with resolving adoption issues. Progress often comes from discovering competence in other dimensions of life. Educational accomplishment, success at work, or breakthroughs in relationships can significantly boost a birthparent's self-esteem. Having made progress in other aspects of life, she may develop the confidence to work through the feelings connected to her adoption experience. This is not, however, an automatic process. We saw earlier that especially competent birthparents often feel the sting of the relinquishment decision most powerfully. For them, the haunting question becomes, "If I am so successful in all these other aspects of life, why was I not encouraged to take on the role of parent?"

The decision to entrust a beloved child to more promising arms requires great strength of character, for it is never easy to stand alone and counter conventional thought. Refuge can be found in returning to one's motives. No one can really know another's intentions; the matter can only be settled in one's own heart. Each birthparent makes the best decision she can in an excruciating context. If she is convinced in her soul that she made the most loving decision, she should be able to defend herself from the torment of guilt and shame, and perhaps even grow to take pride in her decision.

Theologian Lewis Smedes [1993] acquaints us with an obvious but easily overlooked remedy for the pain experienced by those who feel shunned: "The experience of being accepted is the beginning of healing for the feeling of being unacceptable" [p. 107]. Where can birthparents turn to find this acceptance? There are a number of possibilities. Undoubtedly, birthparents profoundly benefit from connecting to peers and other understanding allies. Weary from many critical encounters—some blatant, others subtle—they do well to periodically associate with people who "get it."

This connection is of great importance. Genuine understanding is so rare in their everyday meanderings that birthparents sometimes begin to fear that their adoption experience is beyond the reach of others, that this extraordinary and powerful chapter that colors so much of their perception cannot be shared, that they will forever be lonely.

When they spend time with understanding peers, they redis-
cover their worth as persons and transcend—at least for the
moment—those nagging feelings of alienation.

Hopefully, the adoptive parents whom the birthmother
selected and to whom she entrusted her child are numbered
among the most understanding of her allies. The trust that
adoptive parents extend to birthparents is deeply healing—
and its absence is deeply injurious. In delightfully palpable
fashion, their trust sends the message that the birthparent
is deemed reliable and valuable. Ethicist Christine Pohl
[1999] describes the implications of this sort of hospitality
with great clarity:

> When a person who is not valued by society is re-
> ceived by a socially respected person or group as a
> human being with dignity and worth, small transfor-
> mations occur. The person's self-assessment, so often
> tied to societal assessment, is enhanced. Because
> such actions are countercultural, they are a witness
> to the larger community, which is then challenged
> to reassess its standards and methods of valuing.
> Many persons who are not valued by the larger com-
> munity are essentially invisible to it. When people are
> socially invisible, their needs and concerns are not
> acknowledged and no one even notices the injustices
> they suffer. Hospitality can begin a journey toward
> visibility and respect [p. 62].

Another powerful connection that can help restore a
birthparent's sense of worth is with the child. In the words of
Heather Lowe, an especially articulate birthmother, "The only
thing that will make me feel whole again is a real relationship
with my child." Her insight makes a cogent case for open
adoption. Simply stated, cut off from her son, she is incom-
plete. Connected to him, she is intact. Connection makes all
the difference. An involved open adoption birthparent is

able to get beyond a defensive posture. She is able to roll up her sleeves and relish her relationship with her son or daughter. Repudiating the persistent tug of shame, she celebrates her child's existence wherever she goes. How can the existence of so glorious a child undermine her sense of worthiness? No matter how many disapproving looks she encounters along the way, nothing can alter the fact that she is important to her child, a fact that gives her a great sense of personal worth. A birthparent who is denied this opportunity for involvement, on the other hand, is denied an important avenue toward healing.

Quite possibly the ultimate remedy for the anguish of unworthiness is the realization that we are all God's children. As Smedes [1993] puts it, "The surest cure for the feeling of being an unacceptable person is the discovery that we are accepted by the grace of One whose acceptance matters the most" [p. 108]. He goes on to explain,

> Grace (God's irrepressible love) does not make me feel less; it makes me feel more worthy. Even though it accepts me in spite of what I am, shadows and darkness, it also accepts me for what I am, a rather unique creature of rather unusual worth [p. 122].

When this gracious truth takes hold, it brings great comfort.

Reclaiming the Question

So, after all this discussion, what are we to do with the "how could you" question? We need to find ways to deflect the accusation embedded in its core and reclaim the words as a true question. When these words are posed as a real query, there is an answer. She could because after endless thought she concluded it was the most loving thing to do. She could because she was convinced it served her child better than any alternative. She could because she had great confidence in the adoptive parents. Is this flawed thinking? Or more to the point, is this the thinking of a flawed person?

Most reasonable people will agree that there are many circumstances in which the entrusting of a child to a loving adoptive family is testimony to formidable personal strength, not to weakness. For all the pain and sadness inherent in the adoption decision, many birthparents find an element of triumph. Many would say adoption is both the best and most painful decision they ever made. Gail Cannon, a birthmother blessed with unusual self-awareness, suggests that birthparents who are able to embrace the pain of the experience will likely discover "hidden gifts." Because she was willing to enter the enormity of her pain, she reports that she encountered many unexpected joys. Hers is not the superficial joy of one who denies the pain, but the deep, authentic joy that is only available to those who face their fear. Gail is enjoying the fruits of genuine personal acceptance, and her testimony is an encouragement to many who follow.

How sad that the extraordinary strength underlying the adoption decision is so often mistaken for failure—but that's the way it is with adoption. Adoption seems an almost surreal mixture of pain and delight, shame and pride. Those who ignore the complicated nature of adoption will never understand its astounding depth and its mysterious capacity to enrich even those who endure loss.

Chapter 3

Pathways to Irrelevance: Birthparents as Sinners, Saints, and Suppliers

Most of the paths birthparents travel, it seems, lead to the same destination—irrelevance. Whether they take the high road of noble intentions, the meandering trail of ambivalence, or the superhighway of denial, birthparents all too often end up having little or no importance in the adoptions they set into motion. Some head for oblivion willingly, while others are surprised, once the early commotion subsides, to find themselves consigned to the sidelines. Somehow, irrespective of what participants have in mind at the outset, things often turn out the same. Irrelevance, apparently, is built into the birthparent experience. Or, putting it in slightly different terms, irrelevance is the outcome the system has long produced most capably. Having seen this result for decades, we are accustomed to it and expect little else. For the most part, it has not yet occurred to the system that this is not a desirable outcome.

How does it happen? How do birthparents become irrelevant? How do they so frequently end up with so little standing? Why are they treated as though they are of little long-term importance? These are important, disheartening questions. As is true with marginalized groups of all sorts, the discounting usually begins with a finding of difference. We consider here three common ways in which birthparents are set apart from other, more conventional people, three ways in which they are considered not quite ordinary. It is not a small thing to be deemed out of the ordinary, for once a group is considered unusual in some significant regard, emotional distance is created, and a "we-they" dynamic finds life. It is, unhappily, a small step from "different than" to "less than," and from "less than" to a fearful "watch out for."

Birthparents as Sinners

In Chapter 1, we noted that through the years, birthmothers have been viewed as fallen women. Having veered from community standards, an unmarried pregnant woman was judged a moral failure. In a word, she was a "sinner," and everyone knows a sinner has no moral standing. In the language of Chapter 2, she is not worthy of the consideration upright folks are afforded. A sinner, after all, deserves condemnation and has no basis to assert claims to respectful treatment. She is forever a supplicant; the best she can hope for is mercy.

The stigma attached to "out of wedlock" pregnancy has faded in recent years, but not entirely. I never will forget a call that came in while I was explaining open adoption on a radio program. Taking license in the anonymity of the radio, the caller graphically declared that she did not favor the open approach to adoption. She snarled, "I don't understand all this concern about birthparents. The way I see it, that girl lost all her rights that night she laid on her back and spread her legs." It was a shocking indication that, in the eyes of some, birthparents deserve nothing except judgment. It was a memorable indication that a punitive view of birthparents is still with us.

It's one thing for a judgmental view of birthparents to be expressed in the crass language of the street (or the radio)— these views can be dismissed as uninformed and excessively moralistic—but it's another thing for this line of thought to take on the credibility that comes with psychological terminology. Consider, for example this bold clinical assertion from the 1960s:

> The early family relationships of a girl who becomes an unmarried mother always include problems that were not constructively solved and resulted in a less than normally satisfying pattern of relationships. Many unmarried mothers are emotionally sick. Usually they follow certain basic personality patterns. With unmarried mothers as with all other people, their behavior is an attempt to satisfy their needs and desires. Often they are unable to reach more constructive forms of behavior even though their illicit experiences are not satisfying to them. The lack of continuity in their relationships enhances their need for social relationships and so their problem [Smith 1963, p. 55.].

Over time, the language for those who do not meet expected standards has shifted from overtly moral terms to slightly more subtle psychological phrasing. Descriptive words have evolved from *sinner* to *emotionally sick* to the contemporary *dysfunctional*. As we shall see in Chapter 4, which explores in detail view of birthparents as dysfunctional people, psychological terminology lends stature and credibility to this judgmental perspective. Whatever the language of the day, the meaning is largely the same: Birthparents are flawed persons who have forfeited all claims to respectful treatment. Because they have behaved in objectionable ways, it follows (in the thinking of some, at any rate) that they lose moral standing. As these critics see it, misbehavior deserves a firm response; coddling of any sort is to be discouraged as it only reinforces inappropriate behavior. The thinking seems to be that sinners ought not have any more fun than they have already presumably had.

Characters considered morally deficient rarely generate much sympathy. If things do not go their way, it matters little because they are only getting what they deserve. This critical perspective seldom surfaces in the explicit terms of the radio caller. More often, this viewpoint exists as an unspoken undercurrent of disapproval that justifies treating birthparents as second-class citizens. This is an important observation, for it means that this theme is elusive and difficult to address and correct. The basis for the community's discomfort and disapproval of birthparents is seldom explicit, yet an atmosphere of disapproval and suspicion surely persists, for birthparents regularly feel its sting.

The vague impression that birthparents are somehow flawed has a powerful, enduring impact. Holding diminished moral standing, especially in comparison with highly regarded but down-on-their-luck adoptive parents, birthparents are not in a position to insist on very much. Very few birthparents begin their adoptive relationships as moral equals. With the passage of time, fortunately, many become moral peers, but they do not start their relationships with that sure-footedness. The fact that birthparents enter these relationships with less moral status than the other participants means that most of them are quick to defer to the preferences of the others involved. It also means that any congenial treatment they receive comes as a gift or favor, not as something they deserve. Adoptive parents, meanwhile, are forever commended for "the good thing" they have done. The "good thing" is presumably a reference to their willingness to take their chances on a hapless child from dubious origins. When participants arrive for open adoption's feast of relationship possibilities, birthparents are more often assigned the role of beggar than honored guest.

Birthparents as Saints

Remarkably, when we are not thinking of birthparents as sinners, we may very well think of them as saints. We are impressed by the extraordinary strength of character required of birthparents as they elevate their children's interests ahead of their own, a rare quality in an age that urges us to make sure we get at least our share of the goodies. Observers who pause to think deeply about these matters are touched by this uncommon exhibition of self-control. It occurs to us that the sacrifice birthparents make is no small thing, that theirs is truly outstanding behavior. We find ourselves admiring their maturity and privately wondering if we could be as strong if we were in their circumstances.

As uplifting as this saintly, sacrificial talk is, birthparents should be wary of it. This caution is merited for several reasons. First, it is another distinction, another way that birthparents are set apart and subjected to unusual expectations. Distinctions, even when positive, have a way of creating disadvantageous distance between people. Second, sacrifice is frequently misunderstood and distorted. Yes, it arouses admiration, but it also generates costly confusion. For all its wonder, sacrifice is often taken as a sign of weakness. Consequently, it is not always respected. Third, it can produce unintended results. If we are not careful, sacrifice can be a pathway for the birthparent to remove herself from the adoption picture. If that happens, sacrifice ends up diminishing the child's life circumstances rather than enriching them. Let's take a closer look.

Sainted and Separate

To the extent that we view birthparents as exceptionally sacrificial, we once again set them apart. Certainly the *better than* image is more appealing than the *less than* slant they usually encounter, but it still portrays them as different from others. *Better than* can be just as lonely as *worse than*. If a birthparent accepts this lofty distinction, admitting to subsequent failings becomes difficult for her because she has an image of virtue to maintain. After a while, the image imprisons her. And when we stop to think about it, no one really likes being around people who act as though they are better than others. Over time, admiration drifts toward contempt.

Splendid Doormats

Far more important than these alienating dynamics, however, casting birthparents as saints creates an expectation that they will be continuously and indiscriminately selfless. Enter the no-self birthparent, the adoption participant devoid of substance. This prospect is so serious that we need to explore it in detail.

We are not quite sure what to make of saints—we see so few of them—but mostly we feel pretty good about them. We like having them around because they offer proof that positive forces are still at work in our struggling world. More to the point, we enjoy their company because they are reliably selfless. Sure, they may disturb us a little with their sterling examples, and they may inspire a few pangs of guilt about our comparative shortcomings, but we usually consider them harmless. Their consistency and reliability leads us to the conclusion that they are safe. Since saints are oriented to the needs of others and place little or no emphasis on their own needs, we are confident they won't make trouble. To our delight, saintly persons can be counted on to forgive any mistreatment they might encounter, a marvelous quality that means we do not have to worry about offending them.

The notion of the mature, selfless, giving, thoughtful birthparent is an appealing trap. Each of these pleasant words can carry the subtle message, "She'll make no demands." This high-minded talk of selflessness may be well intended, but we must be careful about issuing anyone an invitation to be extraordinary, for, as we have seen, there is usually a price to pay for choosing a course that is out of the norm. In this instance, the praise of maturity can serve as an invitation for the birthparent to stifle her thoughts and feelings. It can be an alluring invitation to self-discounting. It is one thing for a birthmother to make a careful decision to curb her self-interest so the interests of her child can be advanced, but another thing altogether to be admired into a status that presumes continuous sacrifice.

A Saintly Surrogate

When sacrifice is understood as the eradication of a birthparent's sense of self, adoption can take some unhealthy turns. Sacrifice of this sort can easily become an unhealthy expression of unworthiness. It is more an act of self-annihilation than of self-restraint. To accept or applaud this sort of sacrifice is to join in dismantling a person who is experiencing unusual vulnerability because of circumstances—hardly something for anyone to be pleased about.

Some expectant parents in a selfless mode take on a surrogate mentality. "This isn't really my pregnancy. The way I see it, this isn't my baby—it's Richard and Adrianna's baby. I'm so happy for them." This line of thought may strike some observers as highly desirable, but I fear this approach does the child no favor. A self-abasing birthmother may think she is getting out of the way, but the adopted child may experience this vacating of parental feeling as disavowal. If a birthmother acts as if she does not really exist, it is as though the baby comes from nowhere. Furthermore, if a prospective birthparent is completely self-less throughout a planned adoption, no one is on duty prenatally to love the child. This voluntary erasure of the child's origins may delight some adoptive parents, but it is an act of subtraction from the child's point of view.

The sacrificial perspective can be a trap in another regard. If adoption is identified as the path of sacrifice, does this imply that a decision to raise the child does not entail sacrifice? Obviously, this is a false dichotomy; either decision involves substantial sacrifice. The intimation that a woman who chooses to raise her child herself is selfish is completely without merit.

Understanding the Sacrifice

It seems odd to speak a word of caution about sacrifice and saintliness. Most of the trouble in adoption, as I see it, comes from the other extreme, self-centered thinking. Too many participants in the adoption drama are so caught up with their own needs that they show little regard for the needs of others involved. Since selfishness runs contrary to the spirit of open adoption, most of my efforts in preparing people for adoption invite them to move beyond the constricting effects of self-interest and consider the situation from the vantage of the others involved. When the selfishness of one participant encounters the selfishness of another, the result may be some kind of wary draw. When one party is concerned only about his or her own interests while the other is in a broadly sacrificial mode, there is little likelihood that the process will lead to a healthy, balanced relationship. Unilateral sacrifice can enable irresponsible behavior of many variations. The best results occur when birthparents and adoptive parents alike sacrificially place the needs of the children ahead of their own.

We need to be very clear what the sacrifice of birth-parents is about. I mentioned earlier that the casting of birthparents as saints can create an expectation that they will be continuously and indiscriminately selfless. That is where things get seriously off track. When a birthparent chooses what she hopes and prays will be an improved life course for her child, she does not sign up for a life of never-ending deference to everybody around her. Rather, she is declaring her willingness to contain her personal preferences when it is necessary for the sake of her child's well-being. Plainly stated, the intended beneficiary of her sacrifice is her child, not anyone else. Yes, she will surely make reasonable concessions to the others involved as the adoption moves forward, but these normal reciprocal accommodations that people make in effective relationships rarely reach the level of significant sacrifice.

There is a second clarification of great importance. Although the sacrifice made by birthparents is costly beyond description, it is not all loss and pain. To the extent the decision results from very thorough thought, sacrifice can also be viewed as a personal achievement. Insofar as a birthparent holds high the idea that her child deserves the best life possible, the decision to entrust him to more prepared parents might well be understood as an act of integrity, as a decision to be true to her most vital beliefs. There is inestimable loss, but it is endured for a purpose deemed worthwhile. It is an awareness that sustains many birthparents in moments of doubt. We must not think for a moment, though, that the personal satisfaction that comes with being true to one's beliefs erases the staggering pain of the loss. It does not cancel the pain or even contain it in a tidy, manageable package called "sacrifice"; it just makes it a little more bearable. Because the sacrifice is so emotionally costly, with long-term effects for many people, the birthparent considering adoption should make her decision with the utmost care. Before she sets asides her hopes and dreams, she must be very sure that the gains she hopes to secure for her child are real, not imaginary.

Few people involved with adoption seem terribly bothered by the sacrifices that are asked of birthparents. This happens, I think, because most of the time we take a very light view of sacrifice. In an age of relative plenty, we often think of sacrifice as parting with a little more of our surplus than we ordinarily are willing to part with. Worse yet, I fear we sometimes think of sacrifice as something that borders on foolish. We wonder if someone exercising sacrificial self-restraint is noble or a sucker. How amazing that there can be such a fine line between two appraisals so far apart in meaning.

If we really let the idea of birthparent sacrifice sink in, we would be in awe of it. When we think back to significant sacrifices people have made on our behalf, we are greatly affected by them. The impact of true sacrifice is so powerful it can approach burden status. Understood as an act of integrity, sacrifice is hardly a signal that invites others to cash in on weakness. In fact, if we thought this through more carefully, it would occur to us that someone who has demonstrated the capacity to sacrifice is a person of remarkable determination. If we were looking for weakness to exploit, a person with that much backbone is the last person we would choose to mess with. If saints are the pushovers we sometimes make them out to be, how is that they keep changing the world?

The hazard built into much of the sacrificial talk that birthparents hear is that it leaves them open to the wiles of flattery. It is a beguiling thing for anyone to hear talk of their saintliness, but it is especially powerful for someone who is feeling guilt and shame to be saluted as saintly. Birthparents have to be careful when discussion turns to sacrifice, for the appeal to the magnificence of sacrifice is sometimes a card played by people with an agenda. Too often, the birthparent's sacrificial spirit gets reworked so it serves the wishes of others instead of the child. This is a devastating turn of events. Instead of positioning her to contribute to her child's well-being over the long haul, the expectation of indiscriminate sacrifice can build momentum and sweep her out of the long-term picture.

The trick, then, for those who care about birthparents, is to fully respect their ability to override their self-interest without "reinforcing" this behavior. We must find ways to support the birthparent sacrifice without setting it up as something we expect and hope to see more of. We may choose sacrifice for ourselves, but prescribing it for others is presumptuous. Significantly, it makes sense to speak of sacrifice only if one chooses it for oneself. If a course of loss is somehow imposed on a person, careful use of language requires that we put our description in passive terms and observe that "she was sacrificed."

The original meaning of sacrifice is to make sacred or holy. This understanding puts things in a different light. There's nothing holy about a process that invites anyone to become a doormat for others, for that dynamic diminishes everyone involved. Sacrifice in adoption is not about self-abnegation; it is about intelligently restraining our tendency to consider our own preferences to the exclusion of all others and becoming serious about serving the interests of children. Always, it ought to be about children and finding ways to make life better for them.

The institution of adoption is forever tugged by temptations to cater to the wishes and whims of the adults involved, but it needs to resist these voices if it is to rise above the mundane and profane. As professionals work with prospective birthparents and adoptive parents with all of their strengths and vulnerabilities, the goal is to merge the energies of appropriate self-interest with the tempering influences of genuine interest in the others involved. It is daunting to put this work in terms of holiness, but it helps keep us focused. As long as we are ever mindful of children, we are on course, for the sacrificial love of children is undoubtedly a holy thing.

Birthparents as Suppliers

There is more and more talk these days about the "adoption business" and the "adoption industry." Some people are eager to get beyond an approach they believe has been too senti-mental and hail the dawning of a sensible, straight ahead, no-frills age of adoption. I am not numbered among them.

Certainly there are business dimensions to providing adoption services, and no outfit that wishes to continue offering those services can afford to ignore them. And, with-out question, there is much to learn from the business world in terms of how to listen to consumers and how to honor their intelligence. Effective, ethical business practices can enhance the provision of adoption services, but the practice of adop-tion should never be reduced to a business. The free-market system has worked many contemporary wonders in the world of commerce, but it is a chilling error to apply it to everything that goes on in this world. Some matters of the heart and soul simply are not suited for entrepreneurial pack-aging and distribution.

Adoption is clearly one of these exceptions. There should be no market for children. Children are not for sale. The idea is so abhorrent that we should not use any model that could be viewed as a means by which children are procured for desir-ous adults. To the extent adoption services are organized to satisfy the fancies of adults, they will never enjoy the respect of any who advocate for the respectful treatment of children. The institution of adoption will be on solid moral ground only insofar as it is understood as a service to children.

There are, no doubt, fancier ways to put it, but it seems to me that when adoption is approached as a business rather than a professional service, adoptive parents become customers, children the product, and birthparents the suppliers. Customers, products, and suppliers—not a lot of warmth in that list. Not a lot of dignity, either. By reducing adoption to an impersonal business transaction between adults who are coolly pursuing their individual interests, this approach completely circumvents the fact that adoption is about serving children through the creation of nurturing relationships.

This end run on emotion is not by accident; it is by design. A business approach to adoption avoids the messy inefficiency of building relationships and puts things in the tidy terms of self-interest. In his powerful book, *Civility: Manners, Morals, and the Etiquette of Democracy*, social commentator Stephen Carter observes, "The language of the marketplace, the language of wanting, of winning, of simply taking—the language of self—is supplanting the language of community, of sharing, of fairness..." [1998, p. 180]. With its chilly fascination with efficiency and attaining goals, a business approach to adoption drains the institution of its humanness and diminishes all parties involved.

The view that birthparents are suppliers is quite possibly more insidious than the other perspectives we have been considering. Sinners and saints, after all, are at least particular types of people. A sinner is a flawed individual who has lost his or her claim to respectful treatment, whereas a saint is a sacrificial person who chooses to place no claims on others. Each is regarded as unusual, but they are persons nonetheless. Suppliers, on the other hand, do not fully exist as people. They don't feel, they supply. In this mode, birthparents are subhuman.

I will never forget a comment by a social worker from Nebraska while we chatted during a break in a training session. "People from the West Coast do a lot of advertising in Nebraska," she explained, "because they view our expectant mothers as corn-fed, disease-free stock." Birthparents as stock? On par with animals? Little wonder so many birthparents struggle with feelings of resentment.

Other references to birthparents reveal a disinclination to honor their humanity. Sometimes they are euphemistically viewed as "donors," other times as "incubators" or "conduits" through which babies enter this world. Impoverished pregnant women are unapologetically considered "targets" for creative marketing schemes.

When did we start treating mothers this way? What can we say about a perspective that is only interested in the utility of birthparents? Need we say anything about it? Do we find birthparents interesting because they are of use to a restless market of consumers, or do we value them because they are human? Shall we eye birthparents for their potential as breeding stock, or shall we honor them as fathers and mothers?

Important, But Not Included

We have considered a few of the ways in which birthparents are viewed. The first perspective suggests they do not deserve a place in their children's lives. The second concludes they are harmless and do not have to be taken seriously. The third considers them only momentarily useful. Each of these distinctions is devastating in its own way. The stereotype of moral deficiency erodes social standing, the expectation of sacrifice undermines reasonable self-interest, and an eye toward the utility of birthparents voids the affective dimensions of the experience.

As a result of these views and others like them, birthparents are routinely left out of the adoption loop. Not so many years back, the adoption system—by design—excluded birthparents from continuing involvement with their children by design. Those practices continue in some places, but more often these days birthparents are left out in much subtler ways. It's not that birthparents are actively excluded; they are not actively included. It isn't that they are thought of as the enemy, they simply are not considered important.

Of all the possible conclusions we can reach about birthparents, this is the most amazing. Birthparents may be puzzling or perplexing, but how can such a significant collection of people be considered unimportant? This perception should be turned on its head. The very idea of an unimportant lifegiver strikes me as an oxymoron. It is nonsense. If anything, lifegivers are of great, never-ending importance in the adoptions they set into motion. They are important to their children and everyone involved.

As countless adoptive parents have discovered through their open adoption experiences, birthparents have much to teach. Wise keepers of the institution of adoption ought not be in a hurry to write off any of adoption's participants, much less a group that has this much to offer. Far better that we embrace them and heartily encourage their continuing involvement. If we can't learn from people who have found ways to rework devastating situations and turn them into something constructive, who can we learn from?

Chapter 4

Justifying Distance in Modern Terms: Birthparents as Dysfunctional Persons

It is always interesting to get out of the office and meet with groups wanting to learn more about open adoption. In the early years, these excursions were often difficult because there was so much resistance to our ideas, but these days people are much more receptive to an open approach to adoption. As discussion moves forward, most audiences quickly concur that there are many problems associated with the old secret system, and they agree just as quickly that adopted children are entitled to know the details of their life stories.

It is pleasing to see how much agreement there is, but all the while I know a formidable "yes, but…" lurks in the background. It is the sort of "yes, but…" that has the power to derail all of the potential for health inherent in a system premised on candor. Invariably there is someone in the crowd who can hardly wait to raise a concern. "What you're saying is all fine and dandy, as far as it goes," the skeptic graciously concedes as he or she prepares for a dagger thrust into open adoption's underbelly, "but how well do these ideas work when you're dealing with extremely difficult birthparents? What do you do when the birthparents are highly dysfunctional?" Or, in the memorable words of one especially jaded protective services worker, "What do you do when you are dealing with the cream of the crud?"

Without a doubt, these questioners raise an important concern; but I also believe that in many instances this worry has become an excuse for avoiding the hard but child-honoring work of open adoption. It is a respectable flag to rally around for those who dislike open adoption. Determined to avoid open adoption for a variety of reasons, they eagerly latch onto the one widely accepted reason to move cautiously. They act as though this concern applies to every circumstance and as if there are no ways to relieve it. Sadly, raising the specter of the dysfunctional birthparent has become a sophisticated way for detractors to disqualify the movement toward open adoption and justify the practice of keeping birthparents at arm's length.

Dysfunction Under the Microscope

Dysfunction is a vague but imposing and poisonous word. Most of us are not quite sure what it means, but we know it means something worrisome, and we know that it is best to avoid it whenever we can. When we hear that dysfunction is on the loose, our reflex is to stand back, keep a distance, and take all necessary precautions to protect ourselves. In a word, dysfunction means trouble, and people who know what they are doing usually do all they can to steer clear of trouble.

Bandied about lightly as a convenient catchall term, dysfunction is often overstated in its frequency and severity. Open adoption birthparent Brenda Romanchik reports a variation on the "yes, but..." argument that she routinely encounters. In response to her description of the adoption she arranged for her son, someone in the crowd is sure to comment, "Well, it would be fine to have an open adoption with someone like you, but you are obviously an exceptional person." Even in the face of vivid evidence that birthparents can be reliable—delightful, even—some people seem committed to the familiar comfort of their dreary prejudices about birthparents. Inverting the truth of the matter, they presume that dysfunction is the norm and effectiveness is the exception. In this mind-set, birthparents are, at best, guilty until proven innocent. At worst, they are guilty irrespective of the facts.

A cascade of questions helps us gain perspective on the issue of dysfunction. Aren't we all dysfunctional to some extent? Don't we all do things that are self-defeating—and continue to do them, perhaps on a daily basis, even though we know they get us nowhere? Don't most of us have a few relatives who go off the deep end now and then? Isn't it human nature to make mistakes? Aren't dysfunctional behaviors sometimes understandable or even desirable in the context of crazy circumstances? Might some people who are labeled dysfunctional actually be healthy folks caught up in a dysfunctional system? Isn't dysfunction often in the eye of the beholder? Why are some people considered dysfunctional while others are regarded as eccentric? Are birthparents the only participants in adoption who are sometimes dysfunctional?

If someone is officially dysfunctional, whatever that means, does this status cancel her value as a person? Does dysfunction wipe out a person's importance to her children? Does the label mean that a person is screwed up in every dimension of her life, or might there be some aspects of her life that she manages effectively? Is a finding of dysfunction irreversible? Do people never recover from this affliction? Are these people not wounded in some manner? And if they are wounded, are we not called upon as decent people to respond with compassion and understanding? How are dysfunctional patterns ever broken if opportunities to do things in different ways are never presented?

Aren't dysfunctional people interesting and sometimes even prophetic? Might these disturbers of the universe be good for us? Might they cause us to think a little harder and reach a little deeper? What does my discomfort about dysfunctional people tell me about myself? What will happen to me if someday I am labeled dysfunctional?

Maybe, when we take a little time to think about it, dysfunction is not as exotic or dreadful as we presume it to be. Perhaps it is simply a dimension of everyday living. Maybe there is even an upside to dysfunction in birthparents, for, if nothing else, dysfunction does at least supply a clear answer to the nagging question, "Why was adoption necessary?" It might even be possible that, rather than seeing dysfunction as a deterrent to open adoption, we do well to see it as an important reason to move ahead with an open approach. If dysfunction in some instances has a genetic dimension and is transmitted to the children, continuing access to the birthfamily may be all the more important because it can help adoptive parents more fully understand the issues.

Sometimes, though, we do encounter very troubled birthparents. It is an indisputable fact that some birthparents are difficult to relate to. What are we to do when we encounter especially perplexing birthparents?

Working with Challenging Birthparents

When the movement toward open adoption began, it was necessary to justify the exceptions we made to the assumed policy of secrecy. These days, our default is reversed. In a giant step toward the normalization of adoption, we now presume openness and candor unless there are compelling reasons not to proceed on that basis. And compelling reasons surely do exist. Some birthparents are clearly not candidates for continuing involvement with the adoptive family because they are a threat to the well-being of the children involved. Impulsive, unable, or unwilling to respect reasonable boundaries, combative or violent, they undermine the safety and security of their children. Instead of enriching the lives of the children, they unhappily complicate them. These parents are so accustomed to conflictual interaction with those around them that they have little bent toward cooperation.

Most of the time, it is possible to move ahead with an open approach even though a birthfamily may present special issues. The disruptive powers of dysfunction should not be underestimated, however. The possibility of encountering psychologically unhealthy birthparents is a significant reason for prospective adoptive parents to work through experienced practitioners. These professionals have the training and experience to help organize things in sensible ways, and they frequently have the resources of a larger system to support them. This is not to say that they have all the answers, but they are surely in a position to be very helpful.

An effective system can respond to the challenge of so-called dysfunctional birthparents in several ways.

Treatment

The most basic response to dysfunction, therapeutic intervention, is so obvious that we often overlook it. It is surely the right place to begin. Those who suffer from dysfunctional conditions deserve our best remedial efforts in any circumstance, but they certainly deserve our assistance when their condition threatens their relationships with their children. Happily, many forms of impairment can be successfully addressed through appropriate treatment. Substance abuse, for example, is amenable to treatment, and so are many psychiatric conditions. Basic problem solving can often relieve circumstantial stresses and enable people who are weighed

down with the entanglements of life to function more effectively. Treatment may or may not bring improvement, but
it's worth the effort regardless of its outcome.

When treatment efforts fail to bring relief, there is still
hope that the open adoption process can produce ameliora-
tive effects. Unlike closed adoption, which operates from an
adversarial posture, the open approach to adoption provides
some interesting therapeutic possibilities. Open adoption
can in some instances begin a process of healing. It offering
a fresh start, the exchange of a potentially overwhelming
role for a limited role with more manageable expectations,
and an opportunity to interact with supportive, appreciative
people. If it is too much to hope that a struggling birthparent can get her entire life organized, perhaps she can be
challenged to successfully pull herself together enough to
manage her adoptive relationships. With encouragement and
support, she may handle the responsibilities of open adoption effectively and find satisfaction in her successes. It is
one of those rare circumstances when it makes sense to
encourage psychological compartmentalization.

Systemic Boundary Setting

Responsible service providers know there are times to approach adoption planning with extra caution. In most circumstances, we can happily keep responsibility for most of
the planning in the hands of the participants, where it belongs; but especially worrisome situations call for higher
levels of involvement on our part. For those of us who are
accustomed to trusting the good judgment of participants,
this is an uncomfortable insertion of ourselves into the process. We have worked for years to overcome the oppressive
effects of secrecy, and it feels strange to find ourselves imposing some forms of it on birthparents who are already wrest-

ling with burdensome issues. In every proposed adoption, however, someone must speak vigorously for the child. In those unusual instances when a birthparent shows little regard for the child's interests, the professional, like it or not, must step forward as the child's advocate. Our dismay at the heavy-handedness of our involvement does not alter the fact that some circumstances clearly require sensible restrictions.

Setting appropriate boundaries isn't easy. Depending on the circumstances, it can be an error to either offer openness or withhold it. We may think we are sparing the children unnecessary problems when we shield them from dysfunctional birthparents, but it's impossible to be sure that we are, in fact, making things better, because it's impossible to foresee all the implications of secrecy. Restricting birthfamilies' and adoptive families' access to each other may help in some situations, but it may make things worse in others. Secrecy can offer some degree of protection, but it can also fuel the desperation of the situation. Safety is always paramount, but it comes with a cost. When information and access must be limited for any reason, it is a necessity to be mourned.

The decision to restrict the range of openness options is so consequential that it should not be made by an individual worker. It deserves the wisdom of the entire staff, and the reasons for the decision need to be documented. If our decisions have merit, they can be explained. On the other hand, if we have a hard time explaining ourselves, we very likely have more thinking to do.

Recruitment and Screening of Adoptive Families

Experienced adoption practitioners know that not all potential adoptive parents are appropriate for involvement with difficult birthfamilies. This observation opens a whole new area of specialization in adoption practice. We are accustomed to thinking about children with special needs, but we must also learn how to work with birthparents who present special challenges. The child may be as "normal" as any other, but she is forever linked to a birthfamily who poses unique challenges. That being the case, we have to recruit adoptive families who can effectively relate to these out-of-the-ordinary members of the birthfamily and who can help the child relate to them as well.

Some adoptive families have a knack for working with trying birthparents. The best of them actually enjoy unconventional people and delight in their quirky ways. They may even prefer them over other families they regard as predictable and uninteresting. These stellar families have a decidedly positive outlook that enables them to see the best in people, and the sort of encouraging spirit that actively brings out the best in others. Adoptive parents who work well with unusual birthparents are typically blessed with many interpersonal skills, not the least of which is a lively sense of humor, which they use liberally to reduce situational anxiety. They are matter-of-fact problem solvers who are surprised by little that transpires, and they have the common sense and self-confidence to set and implement reasonable boundaries of their own. Often, these qualities are found in folks who have "been there" and have themselves lived closer to the edge than they might have preferred.

While we actively seek families who can work with unconventional birthfamilies, we do well to actively steer others away from this involvement. As much as we need them, we must watch for unhealthy motivation in prospective adoptive parents. In their eagerness—in some instances, *desperation* may be a more accurate term—to welcome children into their lives, some families volunteer for situations that exceed their emotional and social capabilities. Impatient or fearful that they will never have an opportunity to adopt the sort of child they most desire, they offer to tackle circumstances that are far beyond their aptitude. In doing this, they simultaneously underestimate the challenges involved and overestimate their ability to handle difficulties. Still other adoptive parents respond to perplexing birthfamilies because they feel "called" for various reasons to meet a need. This motivation requires careful exploration, for a dutiful response to difficult birthfamilies can be a joyless thing.

Careful Matching

A whimsical coming together of a birthfamily and an adoptive family is worrisome under the best of circumstances, but it can be a disaster when it involves participants who present special challenges. Chances of organizing an effective adoption are greatly improved when professionals take great care to bring together families who are predisposed toward a positive connection. In the language of service providers, this means extra effort must go into the matching process. As professionals get to know the prospective adoptive parents they are working with, it is important for them to understand not only the range of children the family can accept, but also the kinds of birthfamilies they can work with. An initial assessment of interests and aptitudes is a place to begin. This provides a rugged sense of the sorts of situations a family can tackle, but it is seldom sufficient since most of the time these impressions are stated in very broad terms. More precise information is needed before a match can be made.

When we encounter a birthfamily with especially challenging circumstances at Catholic Human Services, we take some time to carefully identify the nature of our concerns. When we are clear about our professional and personal reactions to birthparents who are considering adoption, we send a written summary of our findings to all of the families in our system who are available to receive a child. This summary is important because it not only provides details about the circumstances, it also offers the worker's "between the lines" impression of things. This is a chance for the professional to set the tone for subsequent interactions, a tone that is both encouraging and realistic. It provides prospective adoptive families with the information they need to make sensible decisions, and it calls on them to exercise their own good judgment. To our great satisfaction, this approach has produced several potential adoptive families in almost every situation we have presented. That means our birthparents have been able to choose the family that they believe is most appropriate from a field of suitable prospects, an opportunity that powerfully affects their level of satisfaction with the adoption.

If a service provider does not have families on hand who are appropriate for a particular birthfamily, networking with other programs is vital so they can expand the range of options for the birthfamily. Ordinarily, geographic distance complicates adoptive relationships, but, speaking frankly, it can be helpful in some of these situations because it reduces the likelihood of casual, unstructured interaction.

After a family who is well-suited to the birthfamily is found, we bring the two families together for a no-obligation introductory meeting. This meeting is important because no one really knows the chemistry of the proposed connection until the participants have a chance to spend some time together. In our experience, these meetings almost always go very well. Personalities and situations that seemed unappealing when described on paper are often offset by appealing qualities that emerge in the course of conversation. The fact that either family can decide not to proceed if it doesn't quite feel right gives them ownership of the decisions they make.

Preparation

Following the no-obligation introductory meeting, we give the two families some time to mull over the idea of coming together to fashion an adoption. It's a major commitment, and it deserves careful consideration. If each declares an interest in moving forward, a second meeting is scheduled to work out the details of their arrangement.

The professional guides the families through this planning process and takes responsibility for setting the initial limits to the arrangement. If the birthfamily has any negative feelings about the limit setting, it's better to direct them toward the professional than toward the prospective adoptive family. Planning an adoption, especially when there are special concerns, is always an artful matter. Some of the steps along the adoption trail are predictable, so planning for those events can be quite detailed. Although there is a tendency for everyone involved to want to "hang loose" as they anticipate the journey ahead, it is wise to be as clear about expectations as possible. Other matters, though, completely defy prediction, so they can only be addressed in general terms. The professional makes notes on the plan as it takes shape, preserving this initial blueprint so it is available as a basis for later review.

Hopefully, far more goes on in the planning session than formulating plans. As the families explore and negotiate their fears and dreams, they learn much about each other and frequently discover more common ground than they anticipated. Their dialogue sets precedents for future discussions and lays the groundwork for trust. This trust-building is at least as important as ironing out the details of the plan. If they can come to see themselves as working together with a common purpose, they have a foundation to work from.

Intermediaries and Maintenance

Some situations may benefit from the insulating effect of intermediaries. We have some experience with this approach from the early days of open adoption, when agencies were reluctant to trust even the healthiest of birthparents. That experience suggests that this approach to adoption is not as pleasing in practice as it seems in theory. For one thing, the amount of time necessary to convey messages and materials between the families makes this a very inefficient way to operate. Very few service providers can afford to provide such an expensive service for 18 years. More importantly, this is an error-prone way for families to communicate. We all know that prospects for distortion increase as more people become involved in conveying a message. Given the sensitivity of many of these messages, it's important that they be as accurate as possible.

Despite these concerns, intermediaries may be useful in some limited circumstances. Occasionally, when the two families have social contacts in common, it is possible to arrange for an indigenous intermediary. Since these intermediaries know and care about both families, they may be able to play a very helpful role. We saw the potential of this approach several years ago in a rather uncomfortable adoption involving a birthmother and an adoptive family who attended the same church. The associate pastor played an invaluable part in helping to relieve the anxiety that flared up intermittently between these two families, neither of which featured any inclination toward compromise. In other rare situations, each family can nominate a person who has somehow earned the trust of the other family to serve as a go-between. In other instances, volunteers—perhaps experienced birthparents or adoptive parents—may be able to fill the intermediary role for a limited time. This arrangement may be helpful if the need for an intermediary is short-lived, but it may be less helpful if the need turns out to be long-term.

After an adoption has been launched—especially an adoption with special provisions—it is helpful to gather for periodic reviews of the plan. These reviews provide an opportunity to fine-tune the adoptive arrangements. They are occasions to work on any problems that have emerged and to celebrate things that have gone well. When relationships are working well and the participants express comfort with each other, it may be possible to expand the amount of interaction between the families. It's not unusual for participants to grow into greater openness as they gain experience and trust with each other. As satisfactory interactions accumulate, more interaction becomes possible.

Attitude

When it comes to interacting with difficult birthparents, attitude is everything. Our attitudes powerfully affect the meanings we attach to circumstances we encounter. How we see things is often more important than what we see. Where one observer sees the "cream of the crud," another sees a devastated brother or sister. Attitude makes all the difference in the way we approach situations.

When I speak of the importance of positive attitudes, I am not encouraging naiveté. Everyone involved needs to be honest about his or her feelings, especially about someone whose actions or inactions might harm a child. It isn't easy to respect someone who has made or is capable of making choices that negatively impact a child—especially a child who is dear to us—but that is the challenge for those who interact with difficult birthfamilies. It is good that we are indignant on behalf of children, yet we must be careful to recognize the vulnerability and enduring dignity of those whom we find worrisome. A positive attitude does not erase hard facts; it enables us to work with these facts in the most constructive manner available. A positive attitude enables us to realize that there is a lot more to a birthfamily than the complications they present.

In dealing with difficult birthparents, we must all doggedly hang onto our respect for their personhood. Rather than highlighting the differences between folks who are doing okay in life and those who struggle, we should make an effort to identify with them. Effective adoptive families refuse to see themselves as better than their birthparent counterparts—luckier than, more fortunate than, maybe, but not better than. When attitudes are positive, there is unwavering recognition that hard times are part of the human condition and that we are all in this together. Because the well-being of the participants is intertwined, effective adoptive parents sincerely want their birthparent counterparts to do well.

At the heart of positive attitudes about birthfamilies is total respect for the need a child has to know her roots. Outstanding adoptive parents are not about to stand in the way of human nature or a child's reasonable need to know. The last thing they want to do is interfere with their child's opportunity to find answers for herself. They want to add to their child's life, not subtract from it. They must believe so deeply in the value of a child's connection to her roots—or, in negative terms, the cost of being cut off from her origins—that they are willing to put up with some aggravation along the way.

The Creative Response

Like the professionals and adoptive parents with whom they interact, birthparents are imperfect, flawed creatures. And, like these others, birthparents also present many strengths.

The fact that some birthparents pose significant challenges to forming and maintaining satisfying adoptive relationships does not undo the extraordinary potential of open adoption, but it does point out the importance of approaching the prospect carefully and fully prepared. A system truly focused on serving children will find creative and sensible ways to deal with struggling participants of every sort. Adoption at its best does not add to the woes of its participants. Rather, it helps them grow in their effectiveness. Although quality adoption practice works hard to provide a secure environment for the child, it is never quick to shrink his world. At its best, adoption is redemptive; it transforms so-called dysfunctional situations into dynamic, constructive relationships that truly honor children.

Part 2

Major Themes in the Birthparent Experience

Chapter 5

Circumstances of Necessity

Birthparents do not turn to adoption lightly. In almost every instance, something difficult, something far less than desirable, necessitates its consideration. None of them grew up with the dream that some day they would find themselves unexpectedly pregnant, have a baby, and promptly pass the care of that squirming, gurgling little person to other, "more prepared" persons. Hardly. Adoption is contemplated because something in that birthmother's circumstance requires its consideration.

Our understanding of birthparents will be limited unless we know something about the circumstances that prompt them to take a long, wrenching yet hopeful look at adoption. A careful examination of the multilayered convergence of family, moral, religious, political, financial, psychological, and relationship factors is very helpful. As important as it is to grasp the complexity of context, however, we must bear in mind that birthparent motivation is never a matter of circumstance alone. Of equal or perhaps greater importance is their interpretation of the circumstances coupled with their appraisal of adoption's capacity to relieve their concerns. In simplest terms, birthparents are motivated toward adoption because of the interplay of circumstances, their evaluation of these circumstances, and their opinions of the alternatives.

Convergence of Circumstances

To understand how circumstance influences birthparents to consider adoption, one must examine the types of circumstances birthparents may face.

Pregnancies that motivate birthparents to consider adoption are usually either untimely, awkward, or unsupported. Alone, any one of these factors can lead to adoption; often, several are at work simultaneously. As we consider the possibilities, remember that some of these factors are much more common than others and that some are far more consequential than others.

Untimely Pregnancy

Pregnancy too soon in life. The heart of this circumstance is timing. The pregnancy has occurred early in life, and the resulting worries are typically twofold: The very young mother may have limited resources, both material and emotional, to adequately meet a child's needs, and the responsibilities of parenting may diminish or delay her prospects for achieving the goals she has set for herself.

Pregnancy too late in life. Less commonly, pregnancy may occur at a time in life when the expectant mother has decided that she is "done" raising children. Aware that her energy level is declining and that her patience is not what it once was, she is dismayed at the prospect of a new round of parenting. She has turned her life energies in other directions, and the idea of circling back to diapers and sleepless nights leaves her discouraged and weary.

Pregnancy too late for abortion. In this instance, an unexpected pregnancy goes unrecognized or is ignored for an extended time. By the time the situation is addressed, abortion may no longer be possible. If the mother is not interested in taking on the challenges of parenting, adoption emerges as her only option.

Not ready for parenting. When asked to describe their reasons for considering adoption, many potential birth-parents of all ages answer that they don't feel ready for parenting. This circumstance is more internal than external, and the expectant mother may find it difficult to express. Her struggle to describe her feelings, however, doesn't mean the feelings are minor—her sense of not being sufficiently mature or prepared to meet the responsibilities of parenting can be very powerful. It is, perhaps, an intuition she has, and experience has taught her to trust intuition. This is such an important factor that we will return to it later.

Awkward Pregnancy

Moral discomfort. Strong religious or ethical convictions are common among birthmothers. She may have strict standards about appropriate sexual behavior, and she frets that a baby is conspicuous evidence that she has violated these standards. Consumed with guilt and shame about her moral lapse, she may not feel worthy of the privilege of mothering. She may view losing the baby to adoption as the price one pays for making a major mistake.

Discretion. In the tradition of Hester Prynne in *The Scarlet Letter*, the temptation to "contain" the damage that might result from the disclosure of moral failure is very strong. When a prominent political or religious figure, for example, helps conceive an extramarital child, the mother may be pressured toward adoption to help maintain the father's or her own public image.

A child too many. Before one has stood in the shoes of a parent, particularly a single parent, it's easy to underestimate the difficulty of the role. An experienced single parent, however, is realistic about the challenge. She knows from prior experience that many of the "call me if you need me" offers of support that expectant women receive are empty, and she knows firsthand how overwhelming the single-parent venture can be. She may fear that she is already over her head attempting to care for one or more children already on board and that another will swamp the family ship and leave no survivors. She is a pragmatist who believes the adoption of one is a better alternative than the loss of all.

Traumatic conception. When the circumstances leading to conception are traumatic, the prospect of parenting can strike an expectant mother as completely unappealing. She may find it emotionally impossible, for example, to raise a child who is the product of rape or incest.

An out-of-character episode. Some pregnancies result from a momentary departure from a woman's usual behavior. A vacation fling, a bout of heavy drinking on the heels of a job promotion, a "walk on the wild side" to shake up a life of boredom are all examples of out-of-the-ordinary behavior that she may wish to put behind her.

Dissatisfaction with the baby's father. A woman's feelings about her baby's father can have a powerful effect on her feelings about the baby. She may feel rejected by the father, or she may be exasperated with him. Perhaps, after his reaction to the pregnancy, she may decide she no longer wants to associate with him. If she is deeply disenchanted with the baby's father, she may find it difficult to forge a satisfying connection to the baby.

Marriage in jeopardy. Pregnancy and the prospect of parenting can sometimes threaten the survival of a marriage. An extremely awkward circumstance—if the husband is not the child's biological father, for instance—may call for a dramatic remedy.

Unsupported Pregnancy

Financial worries. One of the most common factors prompting the consideration of adoption is the lack of adequate financial and practical resources. This is a pressing issue for a high percentage of birthparents. In the most dire circumstances, an expectant parent may not, for various reasons, be eligible for any support from the state. Homeless or close to it, she has few resources with which to meet the challenges of parenting. The choice may come down to living under a bridge or entrusting the baby to adoptive parents.

Familial disapproval. Families vary greatly in their tolerance for an unmarried pregnancy and their willingness to stand by and support a daughter who considers raising her child as a single parent. Most families are able to work through their concerns and trust their daughter's good judgment, but a few are so opposed to the idea of single parenting that they put tremendous pressure on her to set aside her wishes and surrender her child for adoption. For a person who is not physically or emotionally emancipated from her family or who places great value on family harmony, this pressure can be very difficult to resist.

Isolation. Some women lead very solitary lives and face the world with few if any allies. Knowing that she won't have the support from family, friends, or community that most mothers enjoy and rely upon, an expectant mother may view the prospect of parenting too frightening to consider seriously.

Deference to the baby's father. The expectant mother may value her relationship with the baby's father at all costs. Finding herself in the awful position of having to choose between her baby and her man, she chooses to go along with his wishes because she cannot imagine life without him or because she is totally dependent on him.

Questionable competence. An expectant mother who, for example, struggles with mental illness or substance abuse may have her hands full keeping herself afloat as a single person. She may have the presence of mind to question her own ability to parent a child. Or her pregnancy may be a tremendous source of worry for those who look after her. Foreseeing a substantial supportive role they do not welcome, they may pressure her toward adoption.

Recognizing the diverse factors that prompt women to consider adoption, some readers might be wondering how these issues affect the decision-making process. Is it possible, for example, to relieve or remedy some of these problems so the expectant mother can raise the child herself? Or how might each of these circumstances affect the likelihood that a particular birthparent will become fully involved in an open adoption? Others may be drawn to the marketing challenge that this wide range of situations presents. They may wonder how to most effectively present the idea of adoption to these different audiences. Most may find themselves starting to judge the validity of these motivating factors. How quickly ideas spring to mind about what is right and wrong for this vulnerable group. As we reflect on particular items on the list, we may think, "That's a foolish reason to choose adoption" or conversely, "That's a darn good reason to choose adoption." I point this out to remind us of the powerful currents of opinion that swirl around women who face untimely, awkward, or unsupported pregnancies.

Perception and Interpretation of Circumstance

One might think that necessity is an environmental given, but there is much more to the issue. There are many verifiable, factual dimensions of necessity, but these factors only become meaningful in a cultural context. It may be an indisputable fact, for example, that a particular expectant mother is not married, but what that fact means to her—how or even if it influences her decision to keep her baby or consider adoption—depends heavily on cultural interpretation. In some ethnic groups, unmarried pregnancy is completely unacceptable, whereas it's taken in stride in others. Further, the meaning that communities attach to various issues often change over time. Moral acceptance of single parenting has increased in the United States, but some communities are increasingly disinclined to provide financial support to needful families.

As noted above, observers will reach many conclusions about the circumstances that birthparents face. What really matters, however, is what the expectant mother herself thinks about her circumstances, for the struggle with issues of necessity ultimately falls in her lap. She has some important sorting out to do. She must be certain her perception of her circumstances is accurate, and she must be sure that she is analyzing her situation in terms of her own distinct values, capabilities, and interests. In other words, is she reading the factors of necessity accurately? Is she assigning appropriate weight to the elements under consideration? What about timing—is there ever really a good time for a baby to arrive? How awkward is awkward, and can anything relieve or even redeem the awkwardness? Is her reluctance to lean on her family and friends justified? If they are inattentive for some reason, can she find ways to rouse them? If these natural supports are not available, can she find reliable assistance in the broader community?

A circumstance that strikes one person as overwhelming may seem minor to another—the difference is often in each individual's interpretation. This point was made vivid for me in two memorable conversations. In the first, a young couple who had recently discovered they were pregnant was exploring their situation with me. The friendly 17-year-old expectant father did most of the talking. He explained that he had grown up in "a pretty shaky family." He had dropped out of school in the eighth grade and had never been able to hold a job. Warming up to the task of telling his story and ignoring his 15-year-old sweetheart, he explained that he had been drifting about for the last several years staying with various friends until he "wore out his welcome." Completely broke, he was presently staying with her family until "they show me the door."

He wove a pretty fair yarn, and I found myself thinking, "My, he's making a remarkable, truly compelling case for the importance of family stability—I haven't heard it stated this convincingly for some while." I didn't see his punch line coming: "So, you see," he concluded, "if I can turn out as well as I have given the lousy parenting I've had, it's clear that we'll be outstanding parents."

The second lesson in the importance of personal interpretation of circumstances came as an expectant mother prepared to select a family to adopt her child. She suggested that the most important thing was to find a family with a "six-figure income." In all my years of practice, no one else had ever put such emphasis on finances, and I was repelled. To some extent, I was personally offended, because the likes of me—no matter how committed or effective in the parenting role—were summarily ruled out. I immediately challenged her line of thought and asked what a hefty income had to do with effective parenting?

I had unwittingly touched a nerve of shame, and her story was powerful. Through tears and sniffles this woman told me what it was like to grow up in an impoverished, high-crime neighborhood in a large city. Despite relentless daily pressure to set aside her personal standards, she declared, "I never got into drugs and I never prostituted myself." Financial security had meaning for her that had never occurred to me. From my male, middle-class perspective, an emphasis on a hefty income seemed like an arbitrary bid for inordinate luxury. From her perspective, it was a vital hedge against nothing less than the possibility of personal degradation or early death.

These stories remind us that the professionals involved are also powerfully affected by their cultural context. As influential interpreters of the cultural context, it's important for professionals to do all they can to be aware of their biases and control them. There can be no such thing, however, as a completely objective counselor—we all have blind spots, and we all have personal preferences that we may unconsciously defend or promote. Some professionals heartily endorse the social mores of the prevailing culture and encourage clients to comply with them. Others are troubled by various societal expectations and encourage their clients to work around them. This variance of preference and style among professionals creates yet one more variable for expectant parents to take into account. No one should presume for a moment that all adoption professionals are alike, and no one relying on professional guidance should hesitate to seek a second opinion if they sense they are not receiving full and accurate information.

Internal Necessity

As we have seen, necessity has a powerful external and sociological aspect, but it also has a significant internal or spiritual dimension. For many birthparents, necessity has less to do with a difficult situation than with their need to produce an optimal outcome. Responding to perplexing environmental circumstances with resources that others might judge "good enough," the birthmother is not satisfied with prospects she considers marginal. With no intention to judge the decisions of others—what they decide is up to them—she reaches a private conclusion that a plan that may be good enough for others is not good enough for her. She feels it "necessary" to honor this impression, or she may chastise herself for "settling" for something that falls short of what she believes her child deserves. To outsiders, this version of necessity seems more optional than that which is born out of dire circumstance, but many birthparents experience it as more compelling than the circumstantial factors.

When an expectant mother reaches a clear conclusion that, all things considered, her child would be better off in the daily care of another family, she may create for herself a feeling of moral necessity. Her conscience will not let her ignore this finding. It is, by her own standards, a compelling conclusion. As she sees it, a parent's highest calling is to do everything possible to promote the child's interests. Most birthparents choose adoption because they genuinely believe it serves their children's interests better than any other alternative. Part of this notion is based on their conclusion that their circumstances are far from ideal, but the most compelling reason for them to choose adoption is their impression that it stands a very strong chance to create better lives for their children.

How Good Is the Adoption Alternative?

We have seen that the consideration of adoption by potential birthparents is prompted by distressing circumstances and sustained by a personal finding that an extraordinary response is necessary. One more important factor goes into the decision—the need to evaluate the potential of the proposed solution. The birthmother must tackle the question, "How well does adoption work?"

This is no small question. It is complicated, subjective territory that challenges the finest minds in the field. Opinions about adoption range wildly, and proponents of various perspectives are fervent about their views. The most vital question centers on how things turn out for those who are adopted. That question is sometimes answered affirmatively, and sometimes negatively. Almost every conclusion can be supported with some sort of research. Success in adoption, it turns out, is a subjective matter, very much in the eye of the beholder. If the question confounds experts who have closely examined the institution of adoption, read the studies, and interacted with the participants over many years, it is certainly a handful for the person who is taking a serious look at adoption for the first time. Given the diversity of opinion and the ideological arm twisting that goes with the territory, potential birthparents often find that getting objective information is difficult.

As they try to determine the efficacy of adoption, birthparents must also realize that the well-being of birthparents is seldom factored into the public discussion. Appraisals of adoption are far more likely to take into account its meaning for adoptees, adoptive parents, or even the community, rather than consider the effect on birthparents.

Most observers recognize that adoption is not a perfect remedy for untimely, awkward, or unsupported pregnancies. It offers intriguing possibilities for the child—exposure to an enhanced range of opportunities and the delight of an involved father, just to mention a couple—but these advantages are accompanied by significant losses. Popular thinking views adoption as a way for a child to gain a family, but it's just as true that the adopted child also loses a family. A pregnant woman considering adoption for her child needs to consider the ratio of losses and gains posed by the adoption choice. The opinions of other key people in her life about the emotional costs and benefits may be of great interest to her, but it is important that she ultimately reach her own decision about this matter.

Adoptions are not all the same. They take so many forms and produce such varied outcomes that I find it almost impossible to speak in general terms about the ultimate value of adoption. When prospective birthparents evaluate the potential of adoption, they do well to zero in on particular forms of adoption. In addition, they have little choice but to think in terms of probabilities, not certainties. Since no one knows what the future will bring, the only way to realistically approach the future is to think in terms of present motives and future likelihoods. This is difficult, imprecise work at best, and it's subject to a great deal of second-guessing. Some broad aspects of the future may be easy to forecast, but that is usually the extent of our predictive powers.

When birthparents look to the future, they are wise to pay close attention to the character of the people involved in the arrangement. Although the twists and turns of the future defy prediction, personal character hopefully endures. The success of any adoption depends entirely on the quality of the people living it out and the depth of their commitment to making it work to everyone's advantage.

Too often, we reach all or nothing conclusions about adoption. Some people see it as entirely wonderful while others consider it completely awful. Sides are taken, battles are fought. We must resist this simplification of an extremely complex experience. Adoption at its best is often a bittersweet mixture of triumph and sadness. It potentially offers important benefits for everyone involved, but these gains are accompanied by many losses. Women who are thinking about adoption should not base their ideas on propaganda; they deserve a reasonable description of its costs and benefits.

Necessity: A Term That Fits

We can think about the motivation of birthparents in many ways, but I see value in using the language of necessity. On the continuum of choice, the concept of necessity appropriately falls somewhere between voluntary selection and outright coercion. This careful framing of the issue is important, for the degree of control birthparents have over the situation powerfully affects their long-term satisfaction with the arrangement. Adoption results partially from factors that are beyond the birthparent's control and partially from her interpretations of these factors, for which she bears some responsibility. A sense that it is necessary to consider adoption usually starts with the impression that a pregnancy is untimely, awkward, or unsupported. Although necessity often has an oppressive feel about it, there is also an internal version of necessity that moves birthparents to do what they believe is morally correct. This second form of necessity has more to do with the desire to honor the child than with the desire to handle difficulties of circumstance. I want to be careful, however, not to overstate the contrast of these two forms of necessity since, more often than not, they work in tandem to lead to the adoption decision.

Birthparents are a diverse population who wrestle with a great variety of circumstances. Generalizing about them is hazardous, but it's fair to say that they share a common denominator of necessity. Our best chance to understand the birthparent experience is to learn a carefully nuanced language of necessity. The more we understand the intricacies of necessity—typically a mixture of distressing circumstance and resolute determination to do the right thing—the more we will appreciate the endlessly ambivalent nature of adoption.

Chapter 6

Holding On and Letting Go: The Reasonable Ambivalence of Birthparents

Mixed feelings. Do the participants in adoption ever have them? Do they ever find themselves immobilized by conflicting impressions, simultaneously attracted to and repelled by some prospect? The answer is obvious—*adoption abounds with ambivalence!*

For adoptive parents, it comes in waves: first about the very idea of adoption, then about their ability to love "someone else's baby," and ultimately about relating to birthparents. For many adoptees, ambivalence is a powerful ongoing theme, a cloud of befuddlement that follows them as they sort through their amazing life stories. Is it desirable, they wonder, to be different from others? Did they lose or gain through the experience? To whom do they owe loyalty? For birthparents facing the decision of a lifetime, ambivalence often dominates. Bearing in mind that everyone involved in adoption wrestles with some measure of ambivalence, we approach the subject from the perspective of birthparents, since it is an especially powerful aspect of their experience.

As open adoption becomes more common, it is essential for us to explore the breadth, depth, and complexity of ambivalence in the birthparent experience. Open adoption draws, stirs, and in some ways sustains birthparents' ambivalence. Almost by definition, open adoption birthparents—who are simultaneously working to let go and to stay in touch—live with ambivalence; it is inherent in their experience. If we care about birthparents and wish to respond to their circumstances appropriately, we must be clear-minded about this consuming dynamic. Lacking this understanding, we are at risk to compound their confusion.

The Latin root for ambivalence is *ambi,* which means *around, both,* or *on both sides.* Springing from that root, *ambivalence* is a simultaneous attraction to and repulsion from, or conflicting feelings about, a person, action, object, or idea.* A distilled definition might be "conflicting feelings." This notion of internal conflict is important because it points toward the discomfort that typically accompanies ambivalence. We have good reason, in the grip of intensely mixed feelings, to speak of being "painfully ambivalent." As we all know from personal experience, this internal conflict can be extremely uncomfortable.

In the "throes of ambivalence," there is a noticeable absence of motion in any direction. This lack of progress sometimes takes the form of a frenzied flurry of unproductivity—lots of commotion but no forward motion—and other times it operates as stultifying doldrums of inactivity. Wheel spinning or sedentary, the decision maker feels enveloped by confusion and is immobilized. She is exasperated because she is totally stuck, thinking hard, but getting no-

---

* This definition is culled from *The American Heritage Dictionary of the English Language, Third Edition* [1992] and *Merriam-Webster's Collegiate Dictionary, 10th Edition* [1997].

where. She may feel that the harder she thinks, the more stuck she becomes. This feeling of futility tempts her to give up and let a big wave of fate sweep her up and carry her out to sea. Rather than prolong the struggle, she is tempted to yield to the larger forces around her, thereby forfeiting her autonomy.

Some pregnant women contemplating the prospect of adoption struggle with a case of "double ambivalence"—they are ambivalent about the prospect of adoption *and* about the prospect of parenting. They have a mixed perception of each alternative. Adoption both attracts and repels them, and so does the idea of single parenting. These twin ambivalences are obviously closely related. A breakthrough in one struggle can tip the scales of decision making and affect her analysis of the other.

Underlying Factors

Three major factors underlie birthparent ambivalence: moral ambiguity, heart-head conflict (affective-intellectual disharmony), and a nagging perception of necessity. These basic factors, alone or in concert, can significantly afflict potential birthparents and undermine their clarity of direction.

If we cast ambivalence in moral terms, we might say the right course of action is often very difficult to determine—a moral close call. We are ambivalent when a possibility seems to offer nearly equal portions of positive and negative potential. In simple terms, the birthparent who is considering adoption may feel it is wrong to set aside her maternal responsibilities and right to provide a more stable and opportunity-filled circumstance for her child. Amazingly, a single act seems simultaneously right and wrong. This is a genuinely confounding observation. Framed this way, we recognize we are in deep waters, and we are humbled. It appears that ambivalence is testimony both to the extra-ordinary complexity of life, which we sometimes under-estimate, and to our limited skills of moral discernment, which we sometimes overestimate.

Considering adoption, the birthparent usually does not struggle with a dilemma of thought or a conflict between feelings. Rather, she faces a conflict between mind and heart, between thought and emotion—a potent clash between dif-ferent internal systems of perception and appraisal. This gives the predicament something of an apples and oranges quality that profoundly complicates the process of resolu-tion. It is an interior argument conducted in different dialects; her mind presents one analysis, while her heart counters with another. With her usual systems for proces-sing information at loggerheads, she feels bewildered and stymied. How, she wonders with discouragement, will she reconcile such discrepant lines of evaluation?

There is one more significant dimension to birthparent ambivalence; namely, the necessity factor that we explored in the last chapter. Seldom is adoption selected as a true preference—it almost always involves a pronounced ele-ment of necessity. The idea of adoption simply does not occur to pregnant women in circumstances where all is well; it only emerges as a possible outcome when some-thing is seriously askew. Potential birthparents only con-sider adoption because something very powerful compels them to consider it. Under the weight of grim necessity, the choice of adoption sometimes feels to birthparents like an inglorious act of self-preservation—necessity rules.

Something in the human spirit struggles with necessity in almost any form. Intellectually, we know that necessity is a fact of life, yet we yearn for liberation from it. Ultimately, we yield as we must, but it is not uncommon for us to protest, to dig in and resist those things we are compelled to do. We find inventive ways to deny, avoid, delay, ignore, and minimize those factors that move us down a difficult trail. An appreciation of this natural resistance helps us understand the bogged-down feeling that is so often part of the experience of ambivalence.

As stated in Chapter 5, necessity is based on a complex assortment of factors: financial, personal, moral, religious, environmental, and familial, to mention a few. The social environment often compels consideration of adoption, but other times the feeling of necessity is largely the birthparent's own conclusion. The source of this pressure matters a great deal. If outside factors impose necessity, the birthparent is challenged to work through her feelings about this exterior impetus. She struggles with her feelings about authority, independence, and helplessness. On the other hand, when necessity is largely self-imposed, there is room for lively—perhaps ferocious—internal debate about whether this conclusion is merited. She is consumed by the maddening question, "Am I overlooking something, or is adoption truly necessary?" Seldom is she dealing with clean facts. Rather, she wrestles with the subtle interplay of largely unverifiable speculations, predictions, and impressions. Even if she ultimately concludes that there truly is an irrefutable element of necessity in her circumstance, it only launches a new round of internal debate as she begins to work through her emotional response to this depressing conclusion.

Ambivalence Look-Alikes

The three ambivalence factors we have identified as influential to birthparents who are considering adoption—the search for the most morally correct decision, the immobiliz-ing conflict between heart and mind, and the disheartening element of necessity—interact, generating several variations on the ambivalence theme.

Many ambivalence look-alikes feature similar character-istics but actually are very distinct dynamics that we can distinguish by examining them against the backdrop of the three major ambivalence variables. The distinctions are clear-est when viewed through the lens of the moral per-spective, an approach that presumes that most decision makers are searching sincerely for the "right" outcome. Some people will, of course, define right in very simple, pragmatic terms—whatever works is good enough, for example—but others, determined to emerge with clear consciences, will assign high value to moral considerations in their deliberations.

One can feather out variations on the ambivalence theme by examining the tricks that "right" appears to play on those who pursue it. As before, the categories suggested here are neither conclusive nor mutually exclusive.

- **Uncertainty** is often the result of insufficient infor-mation, which in turn makes it difficult to figure out the right course of action.
- **Fluctuation (or Oscillation).** A fluctuating thinker reaches conclusions quickly, but then, besieged with doubt, she sets aside her decision. Right seems elusive and changing. Her pursuit of clarity may be complicated if the opinions of the people around her are similarly fluid.
- **Irresolution.** An irresolute decision maker does not have a clear sense of purpose. Lacking a well-defined sense of what is right in general terms, she is not sure how to decide what is right in the par-ticular circumstance of the moment.

- **Emotional paralysis.** Faced with a perplexing and painful decision, some people shut down. The decision maker may be so overwhelmed that all emotional and intellectual processing stops; or she may know the right course but she is afraid of being wrong.
- **On the horns of a dilemma.** In the grip of a dilemma, we face a choice between equally unsatisfactory alternatives. The decision maker wants to check the box labeled, "None of the above" and faces the nasty task of deciding which prospect is least wrong.
- **Approach-approach conflict.** Sometimes, we must figure out the best of two positive alternatives, a choice between two rights. Although we can take some comfort in the thought that one cannot go too far awry—even if we make the "wrong" choice, it will still be mostly right—this circumstance can be complicated and anguishing nevertheless.
- **The lure of noncommittal objectivity.** The middle ground is often considered the high ground. We frequently regard this posture as fair-minded and balanced. It can be a powerful position. The uncommitted voter, for example, is heavily wooed while predictable constituents are frequently ignored. Sometimes there is drama to be savored in withholding a decision until the last moment. To the noncommittal person, the right course appears to be the middle path, the avoidance of an outcome that some might perceive as extreme.
- **Stalling to delay the inevitable.** In this variation, the element of necessity looms especially large. It is human nature to delay an episode of pain if possible. By exhibiting confusion, the decision

maker may be able to postpone a difficult decision. The decision creates tension for this person
because the right choice is drenched with pain.

- **Stalling to gather strength.** For many of us, processing a difficult, painful reality takes time. It's
not something we can do suddenly. Instinct tells
us to slow down, proceed with caution. We have
to let our emotions catch up with the emerging
necessity. It takes time to come to terms with and
accept what is right; the right thing takes some
getting used to.
- **Hoping for magic.** Occasionally, decision makers
send confusing messages because they are buying
time in hopes that a magical outcome will become
apparent at the last minute. If allowed, they might
be noncommittal forever. As unrealistic as it is
alluring, a magical outcome would be an aggre-
gate of all that is right about each alternative
while avoiding whatever was wrong about them.
- **Breaking difficult news slowly.** People sometimes
give conflicting reports about their intentions,
thereby giving the appearance of ambivalence
when in fact they have already made a decision.
The report of ambivalence may precede announc-
ing a decision that will disappoint someone. As
much as the decision maker would like to keep
everyone happy, that is not possible. She may talk
in circles for a while because she predicts her decision about the right course will be unpopular.

Some Perspective

Most of us do not think a lot about ambivalence, but when
we do we typically view it in negative terms. Often, we react

as if it were a symptom of weakness or failure. We consider it painful and inefficient, surely something to be avoided in our fast-paced culture. There is partial truth in these impressions, but there is more to the story.

Ambivalence is normal and ubiquitous, a familiar companion. In a typical day, many of us respond with a measure of ambivalence to a great variety of circumstances. This is especially true as we approach significant, life-altering crossroads. Although we are not quick to talk about it for fear of the reactions of others, pregnancy decisions are exceptionally prone to ambivalence. They are enormously consequential and are seldom 100% wonderful or 100% awful. These intensely personal decisions pose various ratios of delight and consternation. They are unique and complicated mixtures of pleasure and fear, satisfaction and concern. In high-stakes matters like these, I am far more surprised by the absence of ambivalence than by its presence.

Individuals vary greatly in their predispositions toward ambivalence. Some people seem prone to ambivalence, while others are not. Some automatically see two sides to every issue, whereas others appear predisposed to see and favor one side of an issue. People also have a great range in their abilities to cope with ambivalence once they are in its grip. Some almost enjoy its rigors; others find it unbearable. If we are accustomed and comfortable with ambivalence, we can usually work through it calmly. If, on the other hand, we have little tolerance for it, our distress about our own ambivalence can add to our frustration with the circumstances that prompted it. We may also find that our tolerance for ambivalence may be greater in some circumstances and phases of life than in others.

There are degrees of ambivalence. It is not monolithic; episodes are not alike. Some brushes with ambivalence are brief, while others are enduring. Some afflict us slightly, whereas others threaten to siphon off all clarity and consume all of our vitality. Nor is it unusual for ambivalence to shift its intensity over time. Just as the circumstances of the moment are often fluid, so is the accompanying ambivalence. As a pregnancy moves toward birth, for example, the baby becomes less abstract, a dynamic that may resolve or accentuate the birthmother's ambivalence. As the time of delivery approaches, the wisdom of the heart typically gains influence on its rival, the dispassionate mind.

Although Americans appear to hold decisiveness in higher regard than deliberation, there is much to say in defense of ambivalence. Our affection for action and quick results is of questionable merit, for deliberation is associated with an impressive depth of awareness and respect for the complexities inherent in many ethical determinations. Ambivalence is a more promising frame of mind than oblivion or apathy. In positive fashion, the anguish and persistence of ambivalence signals investment and caring. Also, the enormity of consequences—many of which are unforeseeable—ought to stir a spirit of caution and deliberation. Simplistic thinking is a less-than-satisfying response to the high stakes involved. Ambivalence is a manifestation of realistic thinking and humility. Since the challenges of parenting are indisputably daunting, even in the best of circumstances, these qualities are highly appropriate.

Although ambivalence can be normal and healthy, it can also be destructive and costly. Robbing us of our efficiency and effectiveness, ambivalence can torture our souls and demolish our self-concepts. It can dramatically inhibit our capacity to fully embrace and master the challenges we encounter. Instead of taking charge of our fates, we forfeit control to others. When we are tempted to set aside our competence and resort to flipping coins, it is obvious we have lost confidence in our powers of discernment and creative problem solving.

Does Ambivalence Signal Limited Parental Aptitude?

An important question lurks behind this discussion: What does it mean for an expectant parent, perhaps at the last moment, to veer off course from a proposed adoption and embrace the role of parent? What does her presumed ambivalence mean for her prospects as a parent? This is usually a reasonable and important question, but it sometimes has the sour flavor of disappointment on the part of those who had hoped for an adoption decision. In a quick reversal of opinion, the interest that the birthparent once had in adoption, which various observers previously applauded, is turned against her. "How can she suddenly be so committed to parenthood?" the skeptics ask with suspicion. "What kind of parent could she be when only a few days ago she was trying to unload her responsibility for the child?"

How curious that one moment these critics admire her contemplation of adoption and consider it a sign of maturity, and the next they consider it a cause for concern. The proposed act that one day was regarded as a "loving choice" is the next referred to as "unloading responsibility." This about-face by adoption promoters is not only unfair to the individual suddenly placed under suspicion, it is also transparently shortsighted, as it ultimately undermines their cause. If we can later hold it against the mother that she considered adoption, we create a disincentive for pregnant women to discuss the option in the first place.

This worry about the birthmother's last-minute change of heart reveals a significant misreading of the thinking that goes into an adoption decision. Consideration of adoption, particularly open adoption, ought not be understood as a declaration of disinterest in the child. In my experience, this is almost never the case. If anything, women who consider open adoption are exceptionally committed to their children. Their determination to provide a stable environment for their children and their intention to sustain their relationships with them is a clear statement of deep-seated interest in them. Their consideration of adoption suggests thoughtfulness and the capacity to prioritize the needs of the child— good omens for effective parenting.

Most ambivalence passes with time. People get over it. Somehow, we gradually identify the best alternative, set the project into motion, and move on. The ambivalence of a birthparent who considers adoption but eventually decides to raise her child usually dissipates quickly. Far more often than not, things start to fall into place, momentum builds, and she is carried forward by the usual demands and rewards of life. Babies are uncannily engaging and easily win over people with such modest tactics as wrinkling their brow, sneezing, or a leisurely yawn. In most instances, nature settles the matter by unleashing an almost irresistible hormonal flurry that propels the new mother toward the newborn.

Working Toward Resolution

Living with ambivalence can be frustrating, as can be working with it. As professionals, we want to see our clients enjoy, if not a succession of significant breakthroughs, steady progress. When they bog down in a slough of ambivalence, we can begin to doubt our competence. We wonder why our interaction is not producing more clarity. Where does the professional begin when dealing with lingering ambivalence?

First, we must do no harm. Ambivalence creates vulner-ability. Ambivalent people often welcome outside direction and become easy prey to "helpers" with agendas. There are times, especially when frustration runs high, when the deci-sion maker would love to have some powerful, decisive per-son come along and take the decision out of her hands. A solution like that appeals to the struggler because not only would it bring relief for the pressure of the moment, it would also relieve her of the brunt of responsibility. If things turn out badly, she has someone else to blame. The challenge for conscientious service providers in these circumstances is to resist the easy or efficient outcome and patiently find a way to help the decision maker take responsibility for her life and the life of her child.

In their attempts to support proposed adoptions, some practitioners unwittingly engender ambivalence by discour-aging birthmothers from enjoying their expected babies. " Don't rub your tummy. Don't talk to the baby. Don't give the baby a nickname. You'll just make it harder for yourself." This pitiful advice attempts to stifle and thwart a very natural process of interaction between the expectant mother and the baby. Not only does this advice cruelly deny the baby early affirmation and comfort, it interferes with the mother's opportunity to gather important information about how she feels while interacting with the baby. Ambi-valence is not resolved by blocking feelings; it is relieved by acknowledging and working to understand them.

Second, workers must gain self-awareness about their biases. An expectant mother will surely detect a worker's overidentification with a particular alternative and adapt her interaction to work with or around that preference. As professionals, our reactions to ambivalence can be very revealing. To the worker who is trying to arrange adoption, ambivalence is an exasperating, frustrating impediment to overcome. To the worker striving to help the expectant mother settle on the best decision, it is the central issue, a normal and expected aspect of the work to be done. Wrestling with ambivalence is the creative challenge and the essential service being provided.

Third, we must approach ambivalence with appreciation for its complexity. Ambivalence is no little thing; it deserves a full measure of respect. We must learn to distinguish between the variations on the theme and discern the objects of the ambivalence. Too often, we assume that the expectant mother's ambivalence is centered on the baby, so we overlook the possibility that it is actually connected to her family, the baby's father, the experience of pregnancy, or countless other variables.

Fourth, we must respect the decision maker's analysis of the matter. That means we must work through the difficult issue of self-determination. We need to find ways to constructively challenge her thinking process without imposing our own ideas. This is a tall order. There are, after all, many opinions about the necessity factors, the moral factors, and the quality of thought and feeling that goes into these decisions. If we are doing our jobs well, we will evoke in our clients their own analyses of these complex issues.

Finally, once we have carefully assessed the situation and have a clear grasp of the source of the ambivalence, we can move to problem solving. This is where our awareness of the nature of ambivalence and its look-alikes can help. If the primary dynamic is fluctuation, for example, it is useful to clarify the highest good. When the issue is uncertainty, gaining more information can be very helpful. Faced with an irresolute decision maker, the professional can help her clarify her values and her sense of personal purpose. When the problem is fear, the worker does well to offer support and encouragement. Seldom does stalling require a heavy-handed response from anyone involved, because life itself eventually calls the question with natural deadlines.

Problem solving is an especially important response to potential birthparents when their ambivalence is primarily connected to the necessity factor. With consistently clear analysis, the scales may begin to tip one direction or another. Can the gains that appear to be available through adoption be accomplished through parenting? Can they reduce or relieve the predicted liabilities of adoption? Can the gains that appeared available through parenting be accomplished through adoption? Can the predicted liabilities of parenting be relieved?

Every angle needs to be considered. If the ambivalence partially persists, perhaps we can learn to live with it with greater comfort. We can reframe our view of it, shifting it from (in the view of our go-fast culture) a character flaw to (in the eyes of a thoughtful person) a reflective virtue. Successful resolution of ambivalence requires coming to terms with the necessity factor, and it also means settling the underlying moral issue. If these factors can be addressed with honesty, the ambivalence will most likely be largely resolved in a healthy fashion.

We should be clear about what we mean by resolution. We generally think of resolution in conclusive terms, but it's rarely that simple. How often do we reach a conclusion that one path is entirely correct and the other is entirely wrong? Rather, resolution of ambivalence means we have dignified a difficult circumstance with a thorough process that has involved mind, heart, and soul. We sometimes forget that the *process* of decision making may be at least as important to peace of mind as the conclusion itself. Given that it is not always possible to eliminate some lingering doubt about the wisdom of a final decision, we at least must have confidence in our process of reaching the decision.

Ultimately, the challenge for the ambivalent birthparent is to integrate the wisdom of her mind and heart. It is not as impossible as it sometimes seems, for we are seldom as divided as we presume. Given sufficient time to work things through, the mind and heart usually find common ground and reconcile—almost as though the two internal camps sit with each other and negotiate their differences. The important thing is that, for most people most of the time, ambivalence gradually dissipates. Over time it slowly yields to the integrating powers of a person who remains true to her life purposes.

For all our efforts to resolve ambivalence, we do well to recognize that some traces will likely persist. Perhaps this is just as well. After all, we made the point earlier that there are positive dimensions to ambivalence. In some situations, instead of trying to eradicate ambivalence, we may promote the idea of hanging on to it. For those of us who believe that birthparents have important contributions to make in the lives of their children, ambivalent involvement with the adoptive family is far more desirable that unambivalent detachment. In some ways, the greatness of open adoption is that it does not reduce highly complicated situations into all or nothing solutions. It permits birthparents to both stay involved and move forward. At its best, open adoption acknowledges the ambivalence of birthparents and makes room for it.

Ambivalently Ambivalent

We should not be surprised when we encounter ambivalence along the adoption trail. To the contrary, we should assume it is woven throughout the experience. Although ambivalence has pathological potential, we should not be too quick to think of it in those terms. Whenever possible, it's better that we enjoy the hope and determination that often inhabit ambivalence and learn to honor the depth of thought that it signals. At the very least, we need to be gentle with it. We must not lose sight of the complexity of ambivalence, and we do well to keep in mind that undue pressure for premature resolution may add to the paralysis or, worse yet, produce reckless outcomes. Approached with understanding and patience, on the other hand, it may yield deeply satisfying, creative results.

Ironically, then, we end this discussion with mixed feelings about ambivalence itself. We recognize that it is normal and healthy, but it is also indisputably uncomfortable. And so it is with adoption. Is adoption entirely wonderful? Certainly not. Is it irredeemably painful? No, that's an overstatement. Is ambivalence, then, a reasonable response to the complexity of adoption? Absolutely.

Chapter 7

The Distinctive Grief of Open Adoption Birthparents

That adoption holds many losses for birthparents is hardly a secret, yet few of birthparents are prepared for the grief they encounter. Most find it far more forceful and complex than they anticipated. They are amazed at the intensity of its grip and dismayed at its staying power. Many find their grief confusing and mysterious. However it is experienced, grief is not an insignificant matter. For birthparents, adoption is preeminently about loss and ways to come to terms with it. If they can grow in their understanding of what they are going through, the loss can feel a little less overwhelming.

Grieving is always difficult. The experience is exhausting when we are in territory that is known to us, but it is especially trying when the terrain is unfamiliar. The grief of open adoption birthparents is both familiar and unfamiliar. It encompasses all the standard dynamics and phases of classic grief, but it also involves factors that are unique to the experience of birthparents. They benefit from what they have learned from prior losses, but they need new insights as well.

Defining the Loss

The first task for the grieving birthparent is to define her loss. In most situations in life, this is a simple matter—we know all too well what or whom we have lost and what the loss means for us. For the open adoption birthparent, however, this act of definition is a challenge. Since the birthparent's loss through open adoption is idiosyncratic and out of the ordinary, it is difficult to put into words. How exasperating! One step down the grieving trail, and many birthparents find themselves already confused. How can one successfully grieve a loss that seems to defy definition?

Our effort to understand the unique loss experienced by open adoption birthparents needs to begin with the recognition that it is seldom a singular matter. Birthparents' loss is usually a combination of many losses, the particulars of which matter a great deal.

Lost interaction. In even the most progressive of adoptive arrangements, a birthparent loses the joy of unlimited access to a fascinating, grandly emerging person. This child—nothing less than her flesh and blood and her image bearer—does not forever disappear; but, as happens when a dear friend moves to a distant state, interaction with the child greatly diminishes. Since the give and take of daily interaction is the stuff of life, producing familiarity, intimacy, and interpersonal comfort, this diminution of contact is very consequential and very painful. We take daily contact for granted when it is readily available, but it is sorely missed when lost. It is a loss that significantly shrinks the opportunity for the birthparent to fashion a shared history with her child.

Loss of family structure. When a child leaves the family, a mother loses her sense of clarity about something as basic as the composition of her family. How, for example, does she answer an innocent question about how many children she has? Does she claim the two she is actively raising, or should she also declare the child she entrusted to adoptive parents and prepare to make a lengthy explanation to someone who is quite possibly not all that interested? A simple, everyday question raised by a stranger in an effort to make light conversation can leave her stammering and flustered.

That awkward moment is only a small aspect of this pain. Not only has she lost automatic access to a beloved child with a distinctive personality, she has also lost someone who filled a distinct place in the structure of her family, in terms of gender and position in birth order. As one birthmother said sadly, "My youngest son is no longer in my care." Clearly, she not only missed the child, she also missed the "baby of the family." Another, who was raising her sons, mourned the loss of her only daughter. Each position in the family birth order has unique flavor and status, each position carries an intriguing set of advantages and disadvantages. When we put the loss in these terms, the loss may be subject to redefinition if the birthparent has subsequent children. Whenever a birthparent entrusts a child to an adoptive family, the character and organization of each family is forever altered.

Lost status. Adoption birthparents also endure a loss of a role or status in life. That observation sounds so modest, but it is a statement of enormous consequence. It is, after all, not the loss of just any role, but rather it is the setting aside of what may be life's richest and most challenging role— the daily caregiver affectionately known as Mom or Dad. It is the loss of a revered status in life and of much that defines and identifies us. It is the loss of a fulfilling relationship and the earthshaking intimacy that goes with it. The bond of interdependence between parents and children is deep and essential—no less than primal in the eyes of many observers—and nothing in life can match its emotional power. Nothing can compare with daily family life for its capacity to totally humble us or fill us with pride, to exasperate us or bowl us over with delight.

An amazing, life-shaping role is lost, but open adoption enables the relationship with the "lost" person to persevere, and an extraordinary new status—open adoption birthparent—is assumed. But this novel role is uncomfortably vague, the sort of thing concocted as one presses ahead day by day. There is little we can successfully liken it to; each birthparent must invent her place in the life of the child. Thus, another way to describe the loss is to think of it as the loss of clarity and simplicity, of knowing with ease where one fits in. When one takes on the status of open adoption birthparent, one can expect to blaze a trail through a wilderness of confusing circumstances.

Loss of acknowledgment as a lifegiver. It hurts for the birthmother to go through the experience of labor and birth with little acknowledgment of the event. Seldom is there any public celebration of her wonderfully feminine triumph in giving birth to a beautiful child. Instead of shouts from the mountain top that this woman has brought new life to the planet, we try to keep a lid on the awkwardness of it all. What feels to her like the event of a lifetime gathers only hushed attention. In subsequent conversations, she may be surprised and dismayed to hear the importance of the genetic connection belittled, as so often happens in adoption circles. How painful it is for her to reap so little credit for the magnificence of her child.

Loss of control. The adoption decision can result in a pronounced and painful loss of control for the birthparent. The shift in authority is dramatic and consequential. Early in the adoptive process, she was powerful and much attended to, but with the signing of a few vital documents, her importance to the bureaucrats vanishes. One moment she is highly courted, the next she is ignored. She is suddenly along for the ride rather than at the wheel, demoted from star of the show to hopeful tagalong.

Loss of security. A somewhat subtler loss is of the charming illusion that we are taken care of and that somehow things always work out in storybook fashion. The world suddenly feels like a meaner place, where warm feelings and good intentions do not count for much. Feeling defeated by events that were larger than she, the birthparent may lose confidence in her ability to make a difference.

Lost sense of self-worth. In the most discouraging of times, when shame dwarfs all other realities, the birthmother may come to view herself as a loser who deserves nothing but mistreatment. Quite possibly, the aspect of loss with the most devastating long-term effects may be her lost sense of worthiness. Tragically, if a birthmother feels that she has lost her right to respectful treatment, she is a prime candidate for many future losses.

Unique Dimensions of Loss

Spelling out and clarifying the nature of the birthparent's loss can aid her grieving process, but that effort alone does not ensure that her grief will proceed in a normal fashion. Seven identifiable factors set the loss of open adoption birthparents apart from other more familiar losses.

The loss is more oriented to the future than the past. It has more to do with possibilities and potentialities than with tangible experience. This fact has a twofold impact. First, although the birthmother has precious prenatal memories to hang on to, she has few if any that family, friends, and associates share. This adds to her feeling of isolation—she has no funny or poignant stories to review with others as she works through the loss with companions. Second, since most of her loss is tied to the future and what might have been, the loss is imprecise and formless. Since the future is unknowable and the could-have-beens are ephemeral products of the imagination, there is no way to know the fullness of the loss. It is a maddeningly intangible loss of first rate, multidimensional potential.

The loss is routinely underestimated. Although, as we have seen, the loss is multifaceted and profound, would-be consolers nevertheless routinely minimize it. After all, the reasoning goes, no one has died, and life goes on. This minimizing viewpoint brings no comfort. In fact, it confuses the birthparent because to her the loss does not feel like a modest one. In her mind and heart, the loss is massive and all-encompassing. Nevertheless, the reaction of others stirs doubt and she begins to wonder whether she is making too much fuss.

The loss is ongoing. Each developmental stage the child enters brims with novel delights and brings fresh losses. Just as she works out the losses associated with one stage of the child's development, she encounters a new loss as the youngster moves into the next, even cuter stage. This pattern never ends, so the matter is impossible to resolve "once and for all" as she would prefer to do. Equally upsetting, she eventually encounters the unsettling recognition that the child is becoming a different person than he would have been if she had chosen to do the parenting. The part of her mind that entertains could-have-been thinking continually receives new information on which to ruminate.

The loss is in some ways self-inflicted. Certainly, the degree of volition the birthparent feels about having relinquished her rights ranges dramatically. Birthparents experience a strong element of necessity that compel them to consider this anguished decision, but for the most part, the days when women absolutely had to surrender their children for adoption have passed. Nowadays, outsiders usually perceive the adoption decision as voluntary. On this basis, it draws little sympathy. Observers wonder, "Why should you feel bad about something you chose for yourself? If it was such an awful thing, why did you choose to do it?"

The loss presents a paradoxical upside. The consequences of the adoption decision are not all subtraction; it also has real and significant gains. To grieve a situation that brings welcome relief from significant concerns and introduces new friends into one's life feels odd. When adoptions work well, birthparents grow as people, and their overall situations often improve. Enjoying these gains, though, may generate guilt as the birthparent privately frets that her gain may have come at the expense of her child. The mixed outcome stirs confusion: What sense does it make to feel bad about an outstanding outcome?

This question brings us to an important realization. The gains available through open adoption do not neutralize or erase the losses; gain and loss coexist side by side as equally valid dynamics. Adoption is not a homogenized experience that leads to middle-of-the-road emotions. It is both very sad and very satisfying. Incongruent as they may be, these apparent opposites reside in the same birthparent heart with equal comfort. There are times, though, when even the gains feel like losses as the good things a birthparent sees happening in the life of her child remind her of opportunities she was not able to provide.

The loss of open adoption birthparents is largely uncharted territory. With most losses, we can benefit from the experience of others who have preceded us, but that is seldom the case for birthparents. The grief experience of open adoption birthparents is mostly undescribed. Because past birthparents have maintained low profiles, there are few models to emulate. What's more, since so many people seem determined to portray adoption in positive terms, discussion of the downside of adoption and the pain of birthparents is rare. This information gap reinforces the birthmother's feelings of isolation and doubt.

The loss is confounded by pronounced moral dimensions. The decision to entrust a child to adoptive parents is not always respected. Most birthparents are plagued at some time or another with moments of doubt, and they wonder whether their decision was right. Some are deeply afflicted with shame and are inclined as a result to hide from public scrutiny. When the normal grief reaction of denial joins with shame's trademark desire to hide, healthy processing can shut down completely. If she does not resolve the underlying moral question in a positive fashion, the open adoption birthparent is likely to feel unimportant and unworthy. In this frame of mind and heart, she may also feel that she does not deserve her feeling of sadness and does not even have a right to grieve.

Little Understanding Equals Little Support

The distinctive aspects of loss for open adoption birthparents not only pose difficulties for them, they also confound those who love and wish to support them. How does one begin to respond to someone who is dealing with a loss that is future-oriented, underestimated, ongoing, self-inflicted, partially gainful, indescribable, and complicated by moral questions?

Good question. Unfortunately, the answer is as complex as the question itself.

What form does meaningful support take in this situation? If birthparents themselves have difficulty identifying and articulating the loss, it's no surprise that the people around them have difficulty understanding the feelings involved. Would-be supporters of birthparents, of course, bring their own baggage to the arena. Given adoption's legacy of secrecy, people often presume that birthparents want things kept quiet and are hesitant to broach the subject. If supporters are reluctant to bring up the matter, it's unlikely they will be of much assistance.

Many find the entire situation quite foreign to their experience and are unsure of their deepest feelings about the matter: Is their friend's decision to be applauded or concealed? Many onlookers simply cannot get beyond the question, "How could you?" They are by nature incapable of understanding this decision, and they are clueless about how to help.

Occasionally, frustrated supporters turn grumpy because, even if they have some basic understanding of the loss, they are helpless in their desire to bring relief to their grieving loved one. Exasperated by their powerlessness, they may attack the idea of open adoption as though this system of thought were at fault for the pain and confusion. This understandable venting accomplishes little beyond forcing the birthparent to spend scarce energy justifying and defending the process rather than grieving its pain.

The extent of the birthparent's loss often makes others feel insecure. It's not unusual, of course, for deep grief to make others feel uncomfortable, but in this instance it also creates anxiety and uncertainty. Not wanting to provoke new waves of grief, adoptive parents sometimes withhold the really cute pictures of the baby, the very pictures that hold the greatest ability to reassure and affirm. An attentive birthparent is likely to detect this insecurity and may attempt to protect the adoptive parents from it by stonewalling her grief. She stifles her feelings of grief as a courtesy to others. Close family and friends may also feel insecure around her. When they observe the intensity of her pain, they guiltily wonder whether they did all they could to support her during the pregnancy. As a result, they are tempted to hush her expressions of anguish prematurely or avoid her altogether.

Toward Greater Understanding

Hopefully, our efforts to understand the uniqueness of open adoption birthparents' loss and grief moves us to respond to them more effectively. So how do we start to answer that very good question we raised earlier: How does one begin to respond to someone who is dealing with a loss that is future-oriented, underestimated, ongoing, self-inflicted, partially gainful, indescribable, and complicated by moral questions? Five ideas come to mind.

- **Validate the grief of open adoption birthparents.** Their loss is neither imaginary nor minor. Neither is their bewilderment and confusion about their grief unwarranted. It is imperative that this enormous loss be acknowledged and thoroughly grieved; it is not something to be sloughed off or belittled. We must be patient with our support of birthparents, for their grief is not something they can swiftly process or get over.

- **Embrace a learning perspective.** Clearly, no one has the answers to all of the challenges posed by the formidable grieving experience of birthparents. We have a lot to learn. As people who care, we make ourselves available to hold hands and explore uncharted territory, not to explain a scripted process. There is no room for know-it-alls when it comes to birthparent grief.

- **Make the grief tangible.** It is helpful to make grief work, to give it shape and structure. In most grief situations, there is something to be done, but birthparents have little to occupy their attention or hands. It's a good time to start a journal or to fill out Brenda Romanchik's *A Birthmother's Book of Memories* [1994]. Since birthparents have few established avenues to express grief, they do well to create rituals of their own. These homemade commemorative activities can nourish the flow of healing.

- **Fully use the strengths of open adoption.** Open adoption birthparents have some important advantages as they address their grief and move toward healing. Prominently, because of the forthrightness of the open approach, they are less likely to deny the loss. The child is fully available to delight in and also to stimulate the grieving process. The overall openness of the process, hopefully, leaves birthparents open to grief. Importantly, birthparents have access to reassuring information and supportive, admiring people—the adoptive parents.

  Adoptive parents can be exceptional allies for birthparents as they grieve. The inability to conceive a child leaves them distinctly familiar with the depletion and exasperation of loss—they are insiders to the experience. Too, they are highly motivated to see their child's birthparents recover from the loss. They know that their child's quality of life, as well as their own, is significantly linked to the birthmother's success in the project. As a result, they are often unusually tender and patient in their response to these needful grievers, their friends.

Although the birthmother has lost daily access to her child, and the nature or their relationship has changed significantly, she can draw strength and direction from the fact that she is of never-ending importance to her son or daughter.

- **Learn to fully trust grieving as a natural path to healing.** This is a frightening prospect. Instead of trying to control or force the process, however, we do well to simply let it unfold in earthy, organic fashion. In every aspect of adoption, but particularly in the midst of grief, we must respect the positive power of pain rather than deny and evade the subject. Denial of the pain may bring the painful processing to a chilly halt for a time, but the relief is illusory at best.

That we grow in our ability to deal with this important dimension of the adoption experience is vital, for there is little doubt that unprocessed grief can extract a heavy toll on birthparents. It can affect future relationships, pregnancies, and styles of parenting. Well-processed grief, on the other hand, can bring people together. Grieving is difficult and courageous work that ultimately liberates and sets us free. Patient, effective grieving brings growth, depth, and some measure of relief. If we want adoption to produce healthy results for everyone involved, we will continually expand our understanding of the unique grief of open adoption birthparents and grow in our ability to support them more effectively.

Chapter 8

Gnawing on What Might Have Been: Birthparent Regret

In *Secret Thoughts of an Adoptive Mother* [1997], Jana Wolff raises a monstrously important question. Addressing in her imagination the birthparent who might some day choose her for the glorious and inglorious task of mothering, she dares to wonder, "And what will happen when you realize what you've done?" [p. 17]. In this pithy sentence, which reveals both incredulity about the nature of the birthparent decision and a worried hunch that the birthparent may be sleep-walking, she captures the terror adoptive parents feel as they enter the adoption arena. After all, they know first-hand the creeping despair of a household that lacks the laughter of children. They know the sort of shocking irration-ality that this primal emptiness can spawn, and they fear it. Adoptive parents have many fears about their perilous jour-ney, but none run as deep as their fear of birthparent regret, for they know this emotion transcends all others in its power to unravel the best laid plans and annul their long-standing dreams.

Regret is no stranger to birthparents. It is, of course, a reality for everyone, but it is an especially common and prominent companion for birthparents. It may be as modest as a sporadic twinge of forlorn longing or as oppressive as a lifetime of relentless remorse. Whatever the form, intensity, or duration, we can be sure regret is going to make some sort of visit because it goes with the territory. It goes with high-stakes decision making, and it goes with participation in caring relationships.

The New Lexicon Webster's Dictionary [1987] defines *regret* as "the emotion arising from a wish that some matter or situation could be different from what it is. The emotion may be accompanied by sadness, remorse, disappointment, (or) dissatisfaction." It goes on to state that regret "may arise from something done or said or from some failure to do or say something, or be a response to some general situation." I like the simplicity of this definition. In the most basic terms, regret is the sorrowful wish that things could be different. I also like this definition because it stresses the idea that regret is largely a consequence of our own action or inaction. The observation that regret can be "a response to some general situation" is almost tacked on as an afterthought. We feel regret most intensely when it results from our own decisions and actions.

Responsibility and Regret

Although we may certainly regret outcomes that are the result of events beyond our control, there is little self-assault in that form of regret. I believe we feel regret most vividly when it is the consequence of our own decisions; the most painful and powerful version of regret is characterized by personal culpability. *The Oxford English Dictionary* [1959] supports this emphasis on personal responsibility with its definition of *regret* as "sorrow or pain due to reflection on something one has done or left undone." In that light, we recognize that regret emerges after it occurs to us that an important decision we have made and for which we are responsible has not set as well with us as we had hoped it might. That is when regret is most personal. That is when regret becomes a closed circuit conversation of self-blame.

It is a sad truth that many birthparents feel that they have had very little voice in "their" adoption decision. To varying degrees, adoption feels like something done to them rather than something they chose. Not surprisingly, many of them fervently wish things could be different—a position that sounds a great deal like regret. Perhaps it is a minor distinction, but I believe it is more accurate to view their emotion as resentment. Resentment is a response to exterior forces, and it often carries more anger than does regret. Because these disenfranchised birthparents bear little responsibility for the adoption, their anger is more directed at others than it is toward themselves. They may fault themselves for not resisting the adoption plan more successfully, but most of their disappointment, exasperation, and outrage is directed toward others. They resent the people who pressured them toward a particular outcome and regret their own inability to successfully resist these pressures.

Grief and Regret

To understand regret as an especially intense form of grief is useful as we try to comprehend birthparent regret. The origin of the word *regret* comes from the Middle English word for *lament* [American Heritage, 1992]. To feel regret is to feel a loss vividly and wish to the bottom of our toes it was not so. From this perspective, we see regret as a variation of the denial and bargaining dynamics that are inherent in the grieving process. In the throes of either grief or regret, we have trouble accepting the finality of a difficult circumstance. Unable or unwilling to accept our new reality, we continue to dicker with our Maker about possible revisions to the arrangement. The close relationship between regret and grief is important to keep in mind if either emotion becomes problematic over time. We will explore that possibility later in this chapter.

Ambivalence and Regret

Odd as it appears at first glance, our minds and hearts can fully regret and endorse the same action. Are we not, from time to time, glad we did what we did, even as we rue our action and devoutly wish we had not done it? Wondrously made, we simultaneously hold both views, appreciation and abhorrence. This observation suggests that ambivalence may be another aspect of regret. Psychologist Janet Landman notes that "regret does not necessarily follow...mixed emotions, but it does follow from true ambivalence." [1993, p. 138].

Clearly, there is a significant connection between regret and ambivalence. Decisions made in highly ambivalent circumstances are especially fertile territory for subsequent regret. Just as difficult decisions are seldom prospectively clear-cut, our retrospective appraisals of decisions may be similarly complicated and irresolute. Regret is the persistence of ambivalence. It is as though the anguish of the pending decision is still with us, as though the possibilities posed in that original circumstance continue to exist when, in fact, they have elapsed.

Recognizing the link between ambivalence and regret is instructive. Recalling key observations on ambivalence from Chapter 6, we may project that birthparent regret will likely involve ongoing thoughts and feelings regarding factors of necessity, the search for the right course of action, and the bedeviling challenge of integrating heart and mind. If these elements of ambivalence are not largely relieved at the earlier point of decision, regret looms as a future likelihood. Each element of ambivalence can become a springboard to regret.

Although the factors of external necessity—those dismal environmental circumstances that compel a birthparent to seriously consider adoption—are usually beyond her control, she does bear responsibility for her perception and evaluation of these circumstances, factors of internal necessity. Since the interplay between external and internal necessity is complex, it doesn't take much for her to second-guess her analysis of these factors. Did she read the situation accurately? What difference would it have made, she wonders, if she had found ways to eliminate or reduce the importance of these oppressive environmental factors? What if she had more effectively used her influence to gain the support of potential helpers? What if?

Many birthparents conduct repetitive mental reviews of the circumstances that required the adoption choice. Like a dazed tornado victim combing through the ruins of her home, the birthmother patiently picks and pokes at the relevant factors in hope of finding the key to understanding. Sometimes, her critical reviews have a no-win quality about them, especially when she conducts them when her grief feels overwhelming. If she finds that she overlooked some important item at the time of her decision, she might regret the oversight. On the other hand, if she concludes that the factors compelling the adoption decision were, in fact, irreversible, she may resent the nastiness of her life circumstances.

The second element of ambivalence, the pursuit of the right course, can also stir feelings of regret. If a birthparent sometimes felt that "right" was a moving target while she was deciding, she may have that same impression after making her decision. Too, it's entirely possible that separation from the child may alter her moral vantage point and put an entirely new spin on her thinking—adoption may look morally different to her once she has escaped the panic and pressure of the looming decision. And it isn't just her conclusion that she holds up to the light of morality, for she is also likely to consider the way in which she carried out her decision. If she concludes in retrospect that she cut some moral corners along the way—perhaps, for example, taking unreasonable advantage of her momentary power to secure some financial gain—she is a candidate for guilt as well as regret.

The third element of ambivalence is conflict between thoughts and feelings. If a birthparent short-changes either heart or mind in her original decision-making process, she may expect some complaints from that under-appreciated dimension of her self. If, for example, she largely ignores the wisdom of the heart and favors the intellect, the affronted heart will likely offer some unsolicited after-the-fact commentary. On the other hand, decisions that successfully integrate the wisdom of both mind and heart are less vulnerable to subsequent assaults of regret.

Hope and Regret

One more aspect of regret is worth noting. There is a whimsy to regret that makes it almost impossible to control or manage; it dances on the edge of rationality and is entirely comfortable crossing into irrational territory now and then. In this regard, surprisingly, regret is closely related to a more cheerful counterpart in the human repertoire—hope. Regret and hope share several characteristics: an indomitable belief that things can get better, phenomenal resilience, and an imperviousness to the restrictive powers of logical probability. We might say that regret has a mind of its own. In the language of psychologists, it builds on "counterfactual thought." In other words, it is completely comfortable with objectively improbable conclusions. Reason and factual analysis often have little effect on regret. Stating it even more vigorously, there are no doubt times when rational discussion, instead of bringing relief, inadvertently fuels the flames of regret and deepens its intensity. Regret is by nature unconventional and hard to tame, a dreamer in our midst.

Like many other fundamental aspects of the human experience, regret is difficult to encapsulate in a few words. No single definition begins to convey its nature adequately. Nevertheless, it's safe to say that regret can be understood as a complicated convergence of responsibility, grief, ambivalence, and hope that stirs the self-accusatory, sorrowful wish that things could be different than they are.

Variations on the Theme

Obviously, not all bouts of regret are equally gripping. Some of these internal emotional wrestling matches are far more intense and consuming than others. Some rounds of regret are intermittent, whereas others are persistent. In part, this variability depends on personality. Some people are far more prone to regret than others. Accomplished ruminators, for example, are much more likely to experience regret than are folks who, by nature, seldom look back.

Circumstances also vary greatly in their potential to produce regret. Complicated, consequential, and controversial situations—like untimely, awkward, and unsupported pregnancies—are especially rich spawning grounds for regret. Since every possible course of response contains the prospect of significant loss, untimely pregnancy does not offer any regret-proof alternatives.

What's more, each alternative involves several sub-decisions, each of which can stir regret. Consider for a moment a typical succession of decisions that might lead to adoption—the choice of a romantic partner, the assent to sexual intimacy, the decision to continue the pregnancy, the conclusion that adoption is the best outcome, the type of adoption (closed, modified closed, or open), the choice of service provider, and the choice of adoptive family. These distinct and highly significant determinations are lumped together and called "an adoption decision," but it's more accurate to understand the process as a collection of decisions.

Not surprisingly, some of these decisions may stand up to subsequent review better than others. Over time, one might, for example, continue to endorse the style of adoption but rue the choice of service provider. Or, interestingly, one might regret the decision to move ahead with adoption, but truly enjoy the adoptive family. Regret is invariably more complicated than we make it out to be at the outset.

Regret is usually tied to the beginning or end of an experience. Some forms of regret are rooted in the original decision-making process, whereas others emerge from unforeseen outcomes and consequences. Let's consider some of the shapes regret may take for birthparents.

The Regret of the Typical Decision Maker. Regret is a completely natural part of life for all of us, birthparents or otherwise. Even when our decisions work precisely according to plan, moments of doubt are entirely normal. Who has not second-guessed the potential of a former suitor, the decision to euthanize a pet, or the wisdom of a major financial investment? Even our finest decisions seldom bring all gain—they usually have some downside to them. There are times when, for a thousand reasons, we are more aware of the cost of a decision than we are of its benefits, and in those moments we very well may feel regret.

The Regret of the Mediocre Prophet. We are especially vulnerable to regret when things do not turn out as expected.

Irrationally, a birthparent may genuinely feel that she somehow should have known exactly the way things would turn out and feel frustrated with her inability to foresee a sorrowful outcome. Though she weighed the probabilities carefully at the point of decision, she faults herself for selecting a path that eventually led to a more painful result than anticipated.

The Regret of the Astonished Griever. It is impossible for a birthparent who is considering adoption to anticipate the depth of loss that accompanies that decision. The loss almost always proves more intense and prolonged than she ever anticipated, and the visceral anguish of separation can create an overwhelming sense of longing. Intense, relentless grief drives a person to crave relief in some form or another. Frazzled and worn out, and without meaning to, she may find herself entertaining unexpected thoughts about ways to undo her decision.

The Regret of One Who Lives in Isolation. The adoption choice is probably most livable for a birthparent who has a lot going in her life. For a birthmother who lives in a world of limited prospects, however, second-guessing is nearly inevitable. With little else to occupy her interest, her mind continually circles back to dwell on her feelings of emptiness. Numb from watching grueling hours of television in her lonely apartment, she thinks, "There's not much joy in my life. I don't have anywhere to go with my love and my talents. I might just as well be parenting. I can't stand this loneliness. Adoption was a big mistake."

The Regret of the Forgetful. The forgetful regretter cannot clearly remember the circumstances that prompted her adoption decision. It was such an emotionally overwhelming time for her that many details of the situation are fuzzy. All she remembers is that she was in some sort of fog, going through the motions like a zombie. As a result, she is unable to reconstruct her decision-making process and is disadvantaged in evaluating her decision retrospectively. Try as she might, she cannot generate the information she needs to justify her decision and defend herself from the besieging power of second-guessing. In an especially trying form of this dynamic, the regretter not only forgets the details that led to the original decision, she also manufactures a new set of facts that lend powerful but unwarranted support for her regret.

The Regret of the After-the-Fact Flourisher. To their credit, most birthparents move ahead in life and put their lives into excellent order. Having, over time, worked herself into a circumstance of multidimensional prosperity, it may occur to the birthmother that she is presently well-positioned for parenting. She wonders how she could have decided to forego the tremendously fulfilling opportunity to raise a child. She fuels her second-guessing by applying her current advantages to a past decision made in very different circumstances.

The Regret of the Impulsive Relief-Seeker. For many people, an untimely pregnancy is, at the very least, emotionally very uncomfortable. Deeply distressed, the birthmother may seek relief on almost any terms. Once the dust settles and she takes the time to carefully reflect on her adoption decision, it may occur to her that she acted in haste, that she did not give sufficient thought to all the alternatives. She may fault herself for failing to listen to the small inner voice that warned her to proceed more cautiously.

The Regret of the Naive. Overwhelmed by confusing circumstances, and naively presuming adoption services are all alike, a pregnant woman may innocently trust the first smiling face to come along. She may discover too late that the "professional" service she turned to was actually a business in disguise. She resents the "helper's" failure to provide true help, and she regrets not contacting several service providers before enlisting any one's assistance.

The Regret of the Stubborn. Consumed with a spirit of stubborn independence, a birthparent may disdain all outside opinions when she makes her adoption decision. "Leave me alone," she bristles. "I know what I'm doing." Later, a little older and a little wiser, she thinks, "I wish I had included more people in my decision."

The Regret of the Wishful Thinker. We sometimes grow weary of thinking realistically and reject the annoying restraints of practicality. Eschewing the boring confines of earthbound thinking for at least a moment, we begin to believe wholeheartedly in the improbable and the impossible, and we genuinely wonder why things did not work out in magically perfect fashion. Our minds drift irresistibly toward what could have been. Sick and tired of being sensible, we construct a euphoric fantasy alternative to the painful truth. Comparing mundane reality with our idealized outcome, we regret the ways things turned out. It occurs to us that if we had made this or that adjustment, things could have been different.

The Effects of Regret

Regret has a positive function, but we might say it is poorly designed to produce its useful effect. The primary value of regret is to rouse us to take preventive action, but, since regret is an after-the-fact sensation, its warning usually comes too late to be of much use concerning the matter that generated it. Maddeningly, the instruction that regret offers is for next time. To the extent regret can be anticipated, it can help us avoid mistakes—although one can argue that we can never really know how we will feel after making a decision until we have actually made it. To the extent we feel it retrospectively, we experience regret mostly as a form of personal torment. Regret is a tool nature uses to teach those of us who have to learn the hard way.

Although the lesson learned from regret likely comes too late to be of use to the individual experiencing it—at least in the immediate circumstance—it may be of use to others. Some birthparents transform their regret into something positive by directing their energy toward reforming the institution of adoption. Rather than feeling defeated by their frustrations, they find satisfaction in working to improve practices in the field. This constructive channeling of their energies helps them avoid dwelling on their regrets in an unproductive fashion. Not all efforts toward adoption reform are rooted in regret, of course, but some surely are.

For the most part, however, regret is a depleting dynamic that we would rather not have to deal with. Our dislike for regret is what gives it its power. Regret functions as our own private psychic nag, and we will go to great lengths to avoid or quiet this chattering voice that is so bent on reminding us of our historic shortcomings. This internal accuser saps our positive energies and siphons away our optimism. Regret fans the embers of doubt. It tempts us to dwell fruitlessly on what might have been, even though we fully realize that we can never really know where the other path might have led. Unchecked, sustained regret has the power to erode our effectiveness and erase our self-confidence.

One of the worst effects of regret is that it frequently produces isolation. This isolation results from a twofold process. Intensely regretful people are consumed with deep introspection and are not particularly interested in interacting with others. As the regretful person withdraws into herself, others may begin to avoid her. Regret sometimes carries an element of self-pity that others simply do not want to indulge. To the extent that regret-filled decisions are in many ways beyond repair or remedy, the protracted consideration of those decisions feels unproductive.

Second, there is a helplessness about regret that frustrates listeners and taxes their patience. Twenty seconds into a conversation with a regret-filled person, many listeners want to say, "Get a grip," and move on. What's more, they make a mental note to avoid this stewing ruminator until they think she has returned to a more productive mode. Few people have the patience or desire to go round and round the mulberry bush of someone else's regret.

Regret can be a painful way of keeping a vital memory alive. For some, the torment of regret—for all its soul-gnawing anguish—may be better than the formless despair of total emptiness. The missing person remains vivid in the regretter's imagination and exists as an always-at-hand recipient for the many feelings that continually bubble up. Regret may also be useful to a birthparent in defending her from those who criticize her decision as heartless or uncaring. Demonstrable regret proves that her decision was emotionally costly, that she was not in any hurry to part with her child, and that her caring has continued over time. For others, a never-ending struggle with regret becomes a form of penance. Regret is the price they must pay for errors in their pasts.

As much as we dislike regret and strive to avoid it, there are times that we almost seem to volunteer for it. The great Russian author Dostoevsky speaks vividly of the seductive power of regret:

> I would feel a certain hidden, morbid, nasty little pleasure in the acute awareness that I had once again committed something vile that day…and I would gnaw and gnaw at myself…until the bitterness would finally begin to turn into a kind of shameful,

damnable sweetness and, in the end—into a definite positive pleasure! Yes, a pleasure! I stand by that...[1981, p. 7].

Twisted though it seems, most of us will confess there are times when we willingly admit this infamous tormentor into our minds and give him nurture. As we contentedly chew on ourselves in a self-absorbed fashion, our world steadily shrinks and our productivity dwindles. Before long, though, we regret we ever made room for regret, and we resolve to change our ways. Unfortunately, correction is not a simple matter. We may have a difficult time evicting this graceless freeloader whom we find, to our dismay, has spread out his stuff and settled in, contemptuously hunkered down for the long haul.

Two Poles of Regret

Regret presents itself in two major versions, a reflective, wistful form and an action-oriented, repudiating form. These two poles of regret share the heartfelt wish that things could be different, but they are very different in their expression of this wish. A range of possibilities exists between them.

Closely related to grief, wistful regret is mostly passive in nature. It is the sort of beguiling regret that Dostoevsky described with such color and truth. Introspective and soul-searching, wistful regret often exudes the flavor of melancholy. It is an interesting mixture of idealism and realism. While longing for a more perfect world where woeful decisions and wrenching losses would never be necessary, it accepts that losses of many sorts are an inevitable aspect of life. Wistful regret protests life's imperfections and sincerely wishes things could be different, yet it ultimately yields to the power of these imperfections.

Because the prevailing ingredient in wistful regret is acceptance, it creates an aura that is more tender than angry. When outsiders encounter this soft form of regret, they often respond with kindness. Our hearts go out to the wounded person. Few are frightened by wistfulness. On the contrary, most of us find it easy to identify with the wistful sufferer. We have been there ourselves, and we know that the wistful person means no harm. We instinctively understand that she is working her way toward deeper acceptance.

Repudiating regret has a very different feel. It is a rambunctious form of regret that wants to roll up its sleeves and flex its muscles. Not content to sit back and passively grieve the loss, this active form of regret wants to do something about the consuming sadness. Or, more accurately, it is of a mind to undo the decisions that originally set the sadness into motion. If a birthparent is so distraught about her circumstances that she feels she has nothing to lose, she may cast aside her usual restraints and set out with reckless abandon to correct the mistakes that have been made. "How amazing," she begins to think, "that so much loss hinges on something so puny as a signature on a stupid legal form. Perhaps it should be erased."

Repudiating regret is not as amiable or predictable as its wistful compatriot, and this unpredictability deeply worries the keepers of the institution who want to keep things trouble free. Their worries have been magnified in recent years by sensational media coverage of a few of birthparents' efforts to undo the adoptions they set into motion. Repudiating regret is rare, but the fear of it is so great that the mere mention or intimation of regret in any form can cause a crisis. If a birthparent gives voice to her "undoing" thoughts or takes preliminary action to test the waters of undoing, she becomes a very different person in the eyes of the public in general and adoptive parents in particular. In an instant, her status shifts from friend to foe.

I recall a situation in which a rather impulsive birthmother informed the adoptive parents of her 18-month-old son that, after months of unemployment, she now had a job at a fast-food restaurant and that she was going to contact an attorney to overturn the adoption. The adoptive parents responded to this declaration civilly but made it clear they would defend against her initiative to the utmost of their ability. A week later, the job was gone, and she informed them that she was "just testing their commitment." Because they dug in to defend their right to parent their son, she sweetly informed them, they had passed her test. The crisis passed, but where once they had viewed her with trust, they now regarded her with suspicion and worry.

Most birthparents are well aware of the power regret has to frighten adoptive parents and to rouse their defenses. They also know that it is difficult to relate comfortably with adoptive parents who are fearful and guarded. As a result, most birthparents proactively work to calm these fears. Most go out of their way to reassure their children's adoptive parents that, although they may have their wistful moments, they will never undermine the parental authority of the adoptive parents and they will never seek to undo the adoption. Having chosen adoption so their children may enjoy stability and security, the last thing they want to do is create an atmosphere of instability.

This perspective of regret as a continuum between wistfulness and repudiation spares us the error of thinking that it only takes one form or the other. Regret is too fluid to be captured in dichotomous terms. Placing regret on a continuum helps us to see that there may be some middle ground between passive acceptance and active efforts to undo. The middle ground will take different forms, but often it will be some variation of the courses of action mentioned above in which birthparents accept the reality of their own adoptive experiences but direct their needs to act on their feelings toward improving the larger institution.

The idea that regret exists on a continuum may be misleading in one regard, however, so a crucial clarification is important. We tend to think of variations on a theme as being distributed equally over a continuum. When it comes to the regret of birthparents, however, this is clearly not so. Nor is regret distributed along a bell curve, where most of it falls in the middle ground. In fact, repudiating regret is very rare among birthparents, while wistful regret in some form or another is very common. Clarity about this matter is vital. As long as we stay clear about the fact that the great preponderance of birthparent regret is wistful rather than repudiating, we will approach the subject with far less trepidation.

One more observation about active, repudiating regret before we press on: Repudiating regret sometimes seeks to undo the loss of a child by generating another baby. A replacement pregnancy does not threaten adoptive parents, but it is of great concern to other observers. Obviously, the effort to replace a child, whether undertaken consciously or unconsciously, is a false form of undoing. It does not bring the lost child back into her custody, but, for some birthparents, it seems like the next best thing because another child can fill at least some of the persistent emptiness. Replacement pregnancies raise important questions: Have the factors of necessity that compelled the adoption decision been resolved in such short order? Will the identity and uniqueness of the second child somehow be merged with those of the first?

What's a Birthparent to Do?

Regret poses a significant challenge for many birthparents. First, it directly assaults their sense of personal comfort. If the feelings are especially strong and persistent, a birthparent may begin to worry about her emotional stability. Second, she often feels very alone with her feelings because no one seems to want to hear what she has to say. Third, she is not sure about the implications of her feelings for her relationship with her child. What's a birthparent to do?

One of open adoption's great questions is whether ongoing contact with a son or daughter in adoptive care stirs and sustains birthparent regret or relieves it. Perhaps, to varying degrees, it does both. Ongoing involvement is a mixed blessing. It is one thing for a birthparent to walk up the sidewalk excitedly to a meeting with the youngster and another for her to walk down the same sidewalk at the conclusion of a get-together. She is both delighted to see the child's progress and sad that she is not the one to provide his daily care. To the extent that continuing contact fuels her feelings of regret, it makes interaction with the adoptive family less rewarding for the birthparent. If the emotional scales tip mostly toward regret, she may be tempted to disengage. Tempting as that may be, it is not a conclusion to reach hastily because it holds many implications for both the birthmother and the child.

As painful as involvement with the adoptive family can be, particularly in the early stages when the losses are felt most acutely, I believe the path of greatest emotional risk for birthparents is the one that leads them away from the child. It is hard to know how things go for uninvolved birthparents—if they steer clear of the adoptive family, they typically also avoid the professionals involved—but my impression is that many of them suffer the torments of unfinished business. This is not at all surprising, for the disengaged birthparent creates for herself a circumstance much like that of birthparents from the closed system of adoption. We know from countless reports from that generation of birthparents that the suffering that goes with disconnection is great.

On the other hand, in all my years of open adoption practice, I have never heard a birthparent offer the opinion that she wished she were not involved with the adoptive family. This is one decision that does not appear to generate regret. Even in unfortunate instances in which there has been a divorce or a death in the adoptive family, something about knowing what is going on in the child's adoptive family and being able to participate in the experience brings comfort to the birthparent. Our experience at Catholic Human Services shows that birthparents who stay involved have less difficulty with regret than those who do not.

Although ongoing involvement with the adoptive family can help reduce the birthparent's feelings of regret, this involvement does not eliminate the regret. Some regret persists, raising the question, "To whom does a birthparent turn with her complex feelings of regret?" The question is frustrating because, as mentioned above, not many people want to listen to depressing tales of regret.

Ordinarily, adoptive parents are an attentive audience for birthparents, but the one dynamic they have a very difficult time listening to is regret. It alarms them and puts them in a defensive mode. They know that regret can lead to impulsive behavior, and they immediately start to worry that a regretful birthparent might not be balanced or predictable. Further, the birthmother's regret saps the adoptive parents' joy about something wonderful in their lives. They are deeply saddened at the thought that someone else regards this spectacular event as an unfortunate necessity. Awkwardly, they may feel that they have some power to remedy their friend's regret, but they find the remedy—returning the beloved youngster to her care—unthinkable. Thus, their child's birthparent's expression of regret can stir for them intensely uncomfortable feelings of selfishness, guilt, and helplessness.

For these reasons, it's usually better for birthparents to look for relief from their usual inner circle of supporters, from their original service providers, or from knowledgeable therapists. Of these potential sources of support, the original service providers—presuming they are conscientious about their work and interested in the long-term outcomes of adoption—are usually in the best position to be truly helpful.

What are the implications of birthparent regret for adoptees? Truthfully, many adoptees, like to hear about their birthparents' feelings of regret, for this ongoing discomfort testifies to the fact that out of sight does not mean out of heart and mind. It means they have not been forgotten as they fear, but instead have lingered in the consciousness of their first parents. In the minds of some adoptees, it means that each party—adoptee and birthparent alike—has drawn from the well of sadness and that the cosmic scales of emotional justice are somehow balanced as a result.

An attentive birthparent, of course, easily detects these feelings in her child. This awareness of the youngster's pleasure in her sense of regret creates a tricky circumstance. If she underplays her regret, she may detract from her child's sense of being valued. On the other hand, if she overplays the idea, she may instigate insecurity in her child about the permanence of the adoption. She must find the middle course, a challenge that calls for virtuoso management of her emotions. This is where an awareness of the difference between wistful regret and repudiating regret can serve a birthparent well.

An expression of wistful regret that simultaneously wishes things could have been different yet accepts the reality that they cannot be is important and constructive information for an adopted child. With its honest sadness about the losses brought on by adoption coupled with its respect for adoption's necessary boundaries, wistful regret conveys to the daughter or son that she or he is greatly valued without fueling notions the child might have about the birthmother as an alternative caregiver. It affirms both the loving sadness of adoption and its capacity to work to the advantage of everyone involved. It reassures the child that she has always been loved and that she is where she belongs.

An expression of repudiating regret, on the other hand, can frighten a child. What is a child to make of his birthmother's deep grief and her unwillingness to accept the necessity of adoption? Chances are strong that he may feel responsible for her discomfort and feel guilt that he somehow brought trauma into her life. Her unsettledness may leave him feeling insecure about his circumstance. It may burden and depress him. In an effort to relieve his feelings of insecurity, a child may cling to adoptive parents.

Preventing Regret

After immersing ourselves in the complexity of regret for several pages, two major impressions emerge. For starters, the best response to regret is to do all we can to prevent it in the first place. Regret is potentially so disconcerting that preventive work is well worth the effort. The second observation, however, is that no matter what we do to prevent regret, we will never completely succeed in our efforts. Since we will never eradicate regret, we need to enhance our ability to cope with it when it slips through our defenses and takes hold.

Since regret is usually tied to the original decision or to unanticipated outcomes, that is where we should concentrate our efforts. In practical terms, this means we must focus on the early decisions that lead to adoptions and make sure they are sensible and solid. We must do all we can to effectively support adoptions that have been launched so they work to the satisfaction of everyone involved.

Anticipatory regret is an early warning pointing out the importance of proceeding carefully through the decision-making mine field. It reminds us to gather the facts carefully, move judiciously, and pay full attention to the voice of intuition. Not only do we need to think the decision through carefully, we also need to be sure we capture the rationale for the adoption decision in writing so the context of the decision is available later for review. Sometimes, we can see regret coming no matter what decision we make, because there are no pleasing options. When that is the case, we can use the anticipation of regret to brace ourselves for the deep grief ahead and to commit ourselves to maintain a forward orientation toward life. The anguish of regret reminds us of the importance of doing all we can to integrate reason and emotion in our decision-making process.

Those of us who work in the adoption field need to take the prospect of regret seriously. Regret can happen in the best of adoptions, but it will very likely be less debilitating when highly compatible, well-prepared birth and adoptive parents work together for the child's benefit. This means slowing the process and encouraging the participants to think things through very carefully and in detail. And it means we must faithfully preserve the prospect for birthparents to exit from proposed adoptions at the last minute, especially when we sense that avoidable regret lies just around the corner. Although an unrushed pace may initially add to the participants' anxiety, especially the prospective adoptive parents, it serves their long-term interests. Open adoptions that are fully endorsed by birthparents can be wonderful, but it is equally clear that regret-filled open adoptions can be emotionally devastating for everyone involved. It is also important that professionals stay available to help work out any misunderstandings or disagreements that emerge over time.

Our determination to prevent regret reminds us to think again about the importance of involving birthfathers. As they press ahead with their adoption planning, birthmothers often muse about the meaning of all this for the uninvolved father. "Someday he'll be sorry. Someday he'll wish he was part of all this." The prediction has merit, and it reminds us to do all we reasonably can to involve birthfathers.

Coping with Regret

However diligent our preventive work may be, regret always remains a possibility. This is true because regret refuses to be managed. Janet Landman describes the unpreventable nature of regret very eloquently.

> Regret comes about through comparing the actual with the possible.... It's no good telling us that because the possible is unreal it makes no sense to contrast it with what is real. This advice is too literal-minded for the human psyche. We *will* envision the possible, especially when the actual fails to satisfy our hopes and dreams. To do so is partly what makes us human. To do so is what makes us change for the better. It is a good thing that the human

mind is not limited by what actually exists. It is in this capacity to care enough about the particularities of experience to bother to imagine alternatives to reality that we accomplish the task of becoming fully human. Therefore, a full understanding and experience of regret both accommodates and collapses the actual/possible duality. Regret is the possible pressing its hopeful claims upon the actual [1993, p. 263].

Regret can never simply be driven out of our hearts and minds. If we tackle regret in the fashion of harried villagers contending with a marauding lion, noisily sweeping the fields to drive it from the region, we will surely fail. This crafty man-eater will simply burrow underground and evade the drive. Resistant to logic and reason, regret is both elusive and persistent. Some regret almost always manages to slip though the cracks.

So what are we to do with it once we have it? Let's go back to the earlier definition of regret—a complicated convergence of responsibility, grief, ambivalence, and hope that stirs the sorrowful wish that things could be different—and see if the definition presents any leads for coming to terms with the experience.

These major ingredients of regret can work both ways, either feeding the feeling of regret or reducing its power. Taking full responsibility for our decisions, for example, produces the prospect of self-blame, but it can also bring a sense of control and ownership. Grief magnifies our sense of loss and fuels our wish that things could be different, but it also moves us gradually toward acceptance of our painful reality. Ambivalence has us embracing both views, wishing things could different and appreciating things as they are. Hope can prompt us against all odds to try to undo the sadness, but it can also motivate us to make the open adoption work in ways that exceed anyone's expectations.

Let's consider the healing potential in each of these defining factors.

Responsibility. When we accept responsibility for our decisions, we take rightful credit for satisfying results and shoulder our share of fault for disappointments. As we resolve to stand by our decisions, we apply ourselves to take care of them. Our decisions, after all, stand as lasting testimony to our effectiveness or ineffectiveness as persons, so we have a stake in making them turn out well. When I take responsibility for my decisions and actions, I keep my fate in my own hands. Perhaps others have imposed their will on mine in the past, but by taking personal responsibility for my life course I prevent them from remaining powerful in my life. Perhaps most crucially, as we stand by our decisions we blunt the power of the inner voice that accuses us of poor judgment.

Grief. Effective grieving is another important response to regret. When feelings of regret are sustained or even grow over time, we are called to review the grieving process. Has our grieving been interrupted or derailed in some manner? If we have the courage to let the grieving process move forward in its naturally healing fashion, it will eventually bring us to a state of acceptance. The acceptance that gradually emerges from grieving calms the turbulence of regret. It shifts regretful energy from repudiation to wistfulness. We should note, however, that regret is so resilient that occasional moments of regret will return even when a state of acceptance prevails.

Ambivalence. As suggested in Chapter 6, in some instances we may be wise to support the ambivalence that first set the regret into motion. The double-mindedness of ambivalence, after all, is only half bitter, and that may be a more desirable frame of mind than full-fledged, relentless regret. The positive portion of ambivalence gives us something to work with, a toehold to build from as we work to put regret into perspective. Although we seldom think in these terms, I believe ambivalence, even long-standing ambivalence, can be a fully appropriate response to an inherently complicated circumstance.

Hope. Nothing in the human repertoire can match the sustaining powers of hope. When it sustains futile possibilities, hope leads us to squander our emotional energies. When it sustains us in the pursuit of constructive possibilities, however, it has extraordinary value. Hope can comfort a birthmother with the thought that perhaps every good thing she had in mind for her child in arranging for his adoption will be realized or possibly even surpassed. Constructive hope encourages her to keep her love for her child alive and active. It gives her the spiritual strength to persevere when circumstances take some discouraging turns. Hope produces an expectant, forward-looking orientation.

From Regret to Redemption

Deeply spiritual people will try to find a way to redeem the debilitation of regret. Their faith moves them to study their unsettling experience until they begin to find seeds of meaning in it. They use their immersion in the world of adoption as an opportunity to grow in self-awareness. They work hard to re-frame the situation and eventually learn to view it as a challenge rather than as a never-ending disaster. Gradually they come to own the experience as a life-molding chapter in their ongoing story. Those who possess exceptional spiritual maturity—and they are rare—may even cultivate a sense of gratitude for the difficulties they have endured. That is not to say that they come to bless injustice or tragedy—these they continually decry—but they do welcome and absorb the personal seasoning that accompanies the sadness. For those with faith, a measure of comfort can be found in the belief that life has meaning and that, even though our powers of understanding are limited, on some plane there are reasons for the things that happen in our lives.

There is also hope for forgiveness and grace. We are so hard on ourselves when we are consumed with regret. It is admirable to aspire to high standards, but for the sake of our sanity we also need to be reasonable and cut ourselves a little slack. Instead of dwelling on their shortcomings, it is better for birthparents to give themselves credit for having done the best they could in pressure-packed circumstances. Perhaps they can credit themselves for their positive intentions—nothing less than furthering the life chances of a vulnerable child. To the extent they accuse themselves of flawed judgment, forgiveness is necessary. As forgiveness takes hold and bitterness starts to fade, the destructive power of regret shrinks.

Earlier, I made the point that regret has an isolating effect. Isolation only complicates matters, for it cuts us off from responses that might help us keep things in perspective. It is better for persons struggling with regret to stay in social circulation. In particular, one can find relief in constructive fellowship with peers. The best chance that a birthparent who is struggling with regret has to find genuine understanding is to compare notes with other birthparents. Feelings that are not welcomed in most circles are validated among peers. It is reassuring for a birthparent to discover she is not the only person to struggle with regretful feelings, that in fact she has plenty of company. The cursed loneliness that so often accompanies and compounds the struggle with regret is relieved, and the sense of burden is lightened.

Ultimately, regret is more something to be weathered than fixed. Perhaps when all is said and done, there is little more we can do with regret except to learn to live with it with a measure of grace. And that is no small thing.

Part 3

Fresh Perspectives

Chapter 9

Lifegivers:
How Birthparents Fit In
and Why They Have
Enduring Importance

An unusual set of conversations I had with an expectant mother sticks in my mind. She was finishing her senior year of high school and was thinking that open adoption might be the best outcome for her baby and herself. She was a little wary about the prospect, but she was also thoroughly intrigued, almost giddy about the possibilities. The idea appealed to her because, in her blurred-boundary version of open adoption, it contained nothing but good news. Her plan was to "stop by (the adoptive home) every day and enjoy the baby for a few hours." As she saw it, open adoption allowed her to simultaneously set aside all of the responsibilities of parenting while enjoying all of its benefits—a perfect arrangement! Her perspective was different from what I usually hear from expectant parents mulling over the possibility of adoption, and it left me wondering, "What's wrong with this picture?"

This interesting young lady raises some vital, fundamental questions: Just how do birthparents fit into the scheme of things? How important are they, and what is their "rightful" place in the ongoing experience of open adoption? These questions lead us to consider the very core of open adoption. If we are serious about creating open adoptions that are responsive to the needs of everyone involved, we have to grow in our understanding of the part that birthparents play in the continuously unfolding story of adoption. And if we really wish to be clear about their status, we must grapple with the intriguing interplay between parenting and birthparenting. How do these remarkable stations in life overlap, and how are they different?

Parenting involves three fundamental dimensions: giving life, sustaining life, and affirming life. In open adoption, two of these actions are exclusive, and one is shared. The territory is doled out this way: Birthparents are lifegivers, adoptive parents are daily caregivers, and birthparents and adoptive parents together carry forward with the joyful task of affirming the life of the child they treasure. Although adoptive parents can share somewhat in the lifegiving process through meaningful prenatal involvement and by assisting in the birth experience itself, lifegiving is ultimately the distinct domain of birthparents. Nothing can change that fact. Similarly, although birthparents these days are afforded a variety of opportunities to enter the everyday reality of the adoptive family and meaningfully interact with the child, routine daily parenting is the exclusive realm of adoptive parents.

The young birthparent who saw only gain in open adoption was overlooking one of its most important boundaries—she did not recognize the need for birthparents to fully yield to the exclusivity of the adoptive parents' ongoing parental role. She imagined a form of adoption in which she shared in a substantial portion of the daily care, but that vision is different from the usual reality of open adoption. In her defense, we should note that there is some basis for her confusion. Open adoption, after all, does make the boundaries of adoption far more permeable than they were previously; things are much less clear-cut than they used to be. Open adoption recognizes the deep sadness associated with not being able to provide a vital dimension of parenting, like lifegiving or daily caregiving, and does its best to fill at least some fraction of the sorrowful vacuum. Ultimately, though, it does not alter the exclusivity of these two parental capacities. There is no way around the fact that adoptive parents miss the primal satisfaction of lifegiving and birthparents miss the fantastic intimacy that comes with providing daily care.

The Affirming Dimension of Parenting

While giving birth and everyday care are obvious aspects of parenting, the third factor, affirming life, merits some explanation. Although it does not come to mind as a defining aspect of parenting as quickly as do giving and sustaining life, it nevertheless strikes me as a vital dimension of healthy parenting. This affirming function is a matter of unconditional acceptance and unflagging interest. For a young person, it is the sweetness of having magically powerful people in her corner. It is the joy of having older and wiser people believe in her and pull for her success.

Routinely, we hear athletes say of an especially caring coach, "He is like a father to me." The athlete is not suggesting that the coach gave him life or that he does his wash; he is saying that the coach believes in him. When someone recognizes our potential and has faith in us come what may, the metaphor of choice is parental.

In watching children through the years, it is clear to me that every child needs an audience. Little saddens me more than the thought of a child diligently exploring her world with no one paying attention to her accomplishments. Every

youngster needs someone to celebrate breakthroughs rang-
ing from colorful scribbles on construction paper to national merit scholarships. Affirming parents care deeply
about what goes on in their child's emerging life. They are
genuinely pained at the setbacks she encounters and thrilled
about the triumphs she logs along the way. Irrespective
of circumstances, committed parents are irrepressibly
accepting. Parents love us for who we are, not for what we
accomplish. They love us despite our failings.

Irrepressible caring is something that both sets of parents—birth and adoptive—can offer. Caring of this depth
and duration is a great gift to children because it creates a
great sense of security. It settles forever the question of
whether they count. In an age when far too many children
do not enjoy this confidence, a marvelous feature of open
adoption is that it can supply a double dose of undying
endorsement and acceptance. Children take great comfort
knowing that the important people in their lives are in their
corner rooting for them.

As fabulous as this twofold affirmation can be, it contains a shadow element. Sometimes, the behaviors that go
with a birthparent's expressions of continuing affirmation
and interest resemble the activities of ongoing parenting. It
is possible for expressions of well-wishing by birthparents to
be perceived by adoptive parents as intrusions on their
exclusive responsibility to look after the youngster's needs.
The perception of adoptive parents on this matter is crucial.
If a birthparent action is understood as an expression of
affirmation, it is usually welcomed. On the other hand, if
birthparent behavior is seen as parental caregiving, it can
easily arouse discomfort or resentment. This is tricky territory, because the distinction between the two modes of
action can be very subtle. If a birthparent rushes to provide
comfort to a toddler who has tripped, is it the act of a parent
or the reflex of a caring person?

The Continuing Importance of Biological Connections

Because none of the parents involved in adoption can unilaterally supply all three factors as they would no doubt prefer, they must figure out how to deal with their feelings about the dimension they are missing. The avenues of response are countless, but in the most basic form the choices boil down to three: envy the other's capabilities, ignore or minimize the significance of the other, or fully appreciate the other's contributions. The path that participants select will powerfully color the child's life course.

Envy is a shriveling emotion. There is no joy in envy; it is miserly and fretful. Little can match its power to sour the relationship between birth and adoptive parents and foreclose the possibility of mutual gratitude. When envy reigns, individuals exaggerate the importance of their contributions and belittle the dimension of parenting that is beyond them. Their words may suggest that the unavailable dimension is entirely unimportant, but their message is undermined by the extent of their worry about it. Paradoxically, their envy stands as a conspicuous testimony to the importance of the capabilities they wish to denigrate.

For any who have wondered why the home study expends so much effort on the issue of infertility, this discussion provides at least a partial answer. If the hurt and frustration of infertility has not healed to some degree, it will be predictably difficult for adoptive parents to honor and appreciate the importance of the lifegiving role.

More common than envy is denial. The field of adoption has long underestimated the importance of biology. Many of us who are not adopted have been puzzled at the fascination that persons who were adopted through the closed system show for finding someone who looks like them. What's the big deal, we wonder. By our reckoning, too much resemblance to others can interfere with one's march toward establishing a distinct identity. We take our biology for granted. For the adoptee with no link to his birthfamily, however, resemblance means a great deal. It is, plain and simple, a matter of basic biology. When he says, "I just want to find someone who looks like me," he is saying, "I am longing for biological connection. Something is missing. I need biological grounding."

In the heyday of closed adoption, adoption professionals collected only minimal background information from birthparents because environmental factors were deemed so much more important than genetics. This devaluing of the birth heritage left huge gaps in adoptees' understanding of their roots. And, just as adoptive parents are predictably unhappy when their exclusive role as daily caregivers is not fully respected, birthparents are frustrated when their importance as lifegivers is underestimated.

In contrast to the system's historic lack of appreciation for biological factors, it has been happy to stress the importance of environmental factors. Even though it is often inglorious and mundane work, no one questions the never-ending importance of providing daily care for children. It is the sleeves-rolled-up expression of love. Lifegiving is almost always acknowledged and respected at the time of birth, but it is usually treated as a point-in-time triumph. The ongoing importance of lifegiving is seldom acknowledged in adoption. Although we have a strong impression that biological connection carries special meaning, putting this intuition into words is amazingly difficult. The closest we usually get is the familiar saying, "Blood is thicker than water," an oddly phrased but seldom disputed salute to the enduring power of shared biology.

Even those who are deeply convinced of the importance of the biological connection find it extremely difficult to describe. Psychologist and author Randolph Severson speaks to the issue with more success than most. In *Adoption: Philosophy and Experience* [1994], he writes,

> To be and feel inextricably interconnected, to maintain a sense that we are watched over and cared about by those who have come and gone on before us, to believe that not only here in this life but through the generations the circle is unbroken yields a profound sense of comfort [p. 175].

Severson goes on to say

> I also think in addition to the certainty of faith and the consolation of philosophy, there is something called the comfort of kinship, the comfort of belonging to a family that transcends the generations, the comfort of having ancestors whose love and connection to us death cannot erase. I think it is why most of us want to be buried with our families [p. 180].

Sociobiologists offer an interesting perspective on the vitality of the biological connection. They believe in a form of evolutionary programming—*kinship selection* or *inclusive fitness* [Popenoe 1996, p. 166; Wilson 1993, p. 126], in their words—that moves people to favor relatives in the distribution of scarce resources. They suggest that this process of preferential sharing is ingrained in the human psyche to ensure nothing less than the survival of the species.

Though we struggle to find adequate words, there is something undeniably primal, powerful, and pleasing about swimming in a shared gene pool, and there is something visceral about automatic, presumptive, no-holds-barred identification with "one's own." Biological relatedness surely does not guarantee interpersonal harmony, but it is a formidable given in each person's life. Sooner or later, each of us, if we wish to grow in self-awareness, must reckon with our biological antecedents. Biological connection is no trifle. It is inherently meaningful, never something to underestimate or take lightly.

How Lifegivers Fit In

So we are left with the question of what the continuing importance of biological connection means for open adoption. The implications are significant, for our understanding of lifegiving sets the foundation for a rudimentary description of the birthparent's place in open adoption. Keeping in mind that each birthparent will need to adapt her interaction to particular circumstances, let's look at the way lifegivers fit into the open adoption experience.

Ensure effective caregiving. The most basic responsibility of a lifegiver is to make sure the child is in capable hands. Some birthparents believe their job is done when they select effective adoptive parents and entrust them with the responsibilities of daily care, but an active lifegiver believes there is much more to be accomplished. An involved lifegiver carefully selects the most appropriate adoptive family and continues to endorse and support them as caregivers through the years. This support is, of course, appreciated by adoptive parents, but even more importantly, it helps the child feel secure about the permanence of his adoption.

Render an authentic account of the birth story. No one is more qualified to acquaint a child with her birth story than her birthmother, and no one can tell the tale with more color and detail. Only her lifegiver can tell her that she danced prenatally to the Beatles or that she had hiccups every night at 10 o'clock before she was born. It is her story, and chances are she loves to hear it over and over again.

Explain the adoption decision. Adopted children deserve a firsthand account of their birthparents' rationale for adoption. For the involved birthparent, this is not a one-time task—the child will likely press for more details as he grows older. These explanations will mean different things to him as he moves through the various stages of development, so he may drink from this well of information many times as he grows up.

Provide genealogical context. The lifegiver helps the child understand how she fits into the flow of generations. This helps the youngster gain her bearings and make sense of her personal reality. It gives her her roots. Better yet, when prior generations of birthrelatives are healthy and available, the child's birth heritage comes colorfully alive and is available for her to explore.

Validate feelings. So many people are uncomfortable with the pain of adoption that adopted children often learn to deny their feelings of sadness. An involved lifegiver is uniquely positioned to confirm that sadness truly is part of the adoption experience. This validation helps the child trust his own judgment.

Provide affirmation. The involved lifegiver has many opportunities to express and demonstrate her love. Her presence is, in itself, a message declaring her unending interest in the youngster's well-being. Importantly, her involvement declares that the child's existence is not a source of shame, but a source of celebration and delight.

Create a normal circumstance. Adoptions based on secrecy brim with anxiety about the future. Even adoptions that begin with cooperation between the adoptive and birthfamilies carry unfinished business if the birthparents do not stay involved. An involved birthparent absolves adoption of unwholesome mystery. Instead of fantasizing about banished birthparents, the child is free to enjoy a normal relationship with a normal person. Rather than guessing about characteristics in the child that may have a genetic basis, adoptive parents can make a simple phone call to get to the bottom of things. Rather than dedicating energy to the protection of ground-floor secrets, everyone is emotionally freed to enjoy the relationships.

Dovetail with the child's emerging voice. The nature of the lifegiver's continuing involvement is in many ways based more on response than planning. A crucial skill for an involved birthparent is the ability to read the child's evolving needs and interests. As the child grows older, she will increasingly shape the role of the lifegiver by expressing her desires and preferences.

Toward a Sense of Teamwork

For many decades, the closed system presumed birthparents and adoptive parents were natural adversaries and put them on opposing teams. Even today, unless substantial preparatory work is done to shift their mind-sets from fear and envy to affirmation, they are often guarded about each other. They aren't quite sure what to make of each other and drift toward the idea that they will be rivals.

Consider the language of parenting as a small example of the wariness of the two parties. Birthparents and adoptive parents are often touchy about the words *mother* and *father* or comments like, "That's my daughter." The simplest of conversations employing these expressions can offend others and launch spirals of misunderstanding because they claim a connection that is usually considered exclusive. These claiming words are so important and meaningful that both sets of parents tend to stake their claims righteously and unequivocally. Their fervor is based on sacrifice—dramatic separation for birthparents and daily caregiving for adoptive parents—and each feels fully entitled to a bit of deference.

We can avoid many of these misunderstandings if we keep the interplay of the three basic dimensions of parenting in mind. This is a challenge, however, for our use of language in this area is imprecise. I have spoken of lifegiving, caregiving, and affirmation as vital aspects under the umbrella of parenting. The trouble is that what I have called caregiving is usually referred to as "parenting." Obviously, then, there is room for confusion about "parenting" because we are using the word in different ways. When we speak of parenting, do we have its broadest meaning in mind, or are we thinking of its more particular caregiving application? This confusion is discouraging. Whatever clarity of thought we might gain from describing and distinguishing the basic roles of birthparents and adoptive parents is threatened by our imprecise habits of language.

We noted earlier that neither the birthparents nor the adoptive parents can unilaterally provide all three dimensions of parenting. They may try to ignore or belittle the missing dimension, but these strategies will shortchange children every time. Adoptive parents will be hindered in their ability to fully understand their children if they do not have information from the birthparents, and birthparents will likely have no meaningful access to their children unless they have positive relationships with the adoptive parents.

Lifegivers and caregivers do not share or compete for the same roles; they have separate and distinct responsibilities to meet. When birthparents select open adoption as the best course for their children, they pass the role of active-duty parenting to the adoptive parents and take on the responsibilities of active duty lifegivers for themselves. With this fundamental understanding, birthparents and adoptive parents are not rivals, they are compatriots in the exciting task of shaping the life of a much loved child. They are co-creators and sustainers of the child's ongoing reality.

If anyone in the parental constellation is unavailable to the youngster, he will miss valuable affirmation. He needs both sets of parents. He counts on the steadiness of his everyday parents and savors the continuing interest of his lifegivers. And, of course, it is no secret that children enjoy all the affirmation they can garner. What can be sweeter than to have all of the important people in our lives rooting for us?

When birthparents and adoptive parents are clear about their statuses as lifegivers and caregivers, there is very little chance the children will experience confusion. Since the most common and enduring misapprehension of open adoption is that it confuses the children, this is an extremely important observation. Our 20 years of experience at Catholic Human Services indicates that children are not confused by the involvement of birthparents. To the contrary, open adoption kids are especially well-positioned to figure things out. They know with perfect clarity who takes care of them every day, and they know with equal clarity who gave them life. They also know full well which people in their lives are expressing special interest in them. Even in arrangements where boundaries haven't been very well-defined, our experience suggests that the children have been consistently clear about the way they relate to the various parties involved. As we move toward greater clarity about the basic roles of the parental figures, the likelihood that kids will experience confusion becomes even more remote.

To produce the best results for children, birthparents and adoptive parents must recognize their interdependence. Each will fill their own unique position most successfully if they are in sync with their parental counterparts. Hopefully, we will not let envious or possessive thinking cloud our perceptions and interfere with our pursuit of teamwork. Open adoptions grow in satisfaction as we clearly distinguish exclusive responsibilities from shared privileges. When the exclusive aspects of parenting are affirmed, respected, and supported, adoptive parents and birthparents have no sense of rivalry. When their inter-dependence is embraced rather than resented, adoptive parents and birthparents create loving, cooperative circum-stances for their children. And when children feel the unconditional love and affection of all the crucial contrib-utors to their life stories, they are positioned to thrive.

Chapter 10

Open Adoption's Holy Grail: The Birthparent Role

Many of us in the open adoption movement are eager to find a way to adequately describe the role of birthparents in the open system. We search for it zealously—it is our Holy Grail.

If Indiana Jones ever roamed the realm of open adoption, this would be his quest. If only he or some other charismatic crusader would find a way to define the birthparent role, we could make open adoption less mysterious for everyone, participants and nonparticipants alike. If we could spell out a clear script for appropriate birthparent behavior in the context of ongoing open adoption, life would be good. We could spare birthparents the humbling process of trial and error they presently undergo and help them to hit the ground running. We could help them feel more at ease in the arrangement, since a certain amount of security comes with having a role to fill—one feels entitled to do what one is doing, after all, because it is the sort of thing that people in this role are expected to do. And if we could adequately describe how birthparents fit into the scheme of things, since the roles of the participants are all interconnected, it would have the happy effect of helping adoptive parents and the children understand their parts better as well.

Although I have searched as vigorously for the grail as most, it is increasingly clear to me that Michigan Gritter, for one, is not going to find it. I have begun to think that we are pursuing a phantom. What's more, I am no longer sure that I want to find it even if it does exist. That thought came to mind as I read a comment by Eugene Peterson in *The Wisdom of Each Other: A Conversation Between Spiritual Friends* [1998]. This wise pastor and author muses,

> The moment an aspect of Christian living (human life for that matter) is defined as a role, it is distorted, debased—and eventually destroyed. We are brothers and sisters with one another, friends and lovers, saints and sinners [p. 67].

Obviously, Peterson is not talking about adoption, but I think his insight applies to a variety of circumstances. Anytime we reduce our interaction with others to playing out of preordained scripts, we lose a great deal. Clarity about our role may relieve some of our worries about fitting in, but it may cost us our sense of joy about participating in an adventure of our own creation. There's a chance that the effort to fill a role might deaden our creative impulses and dull our spontaneity. There is also some hazard that carefully explained role distinctions may box us into egocentric concerns about little more than our own role in the drama. Rather than helping us discover how we fit together, these distinctions may keep us comfortably apart and deny us the opportunity to forge a shared understanding of who we are as connected individuals.

My primary worry about approaching the birthparent experience in open adoption from a role perspective is that this mode of thought emphasizes the importance of function over the essential worth birthparents hold as persons. It is an echo of the view that sees birthparents as suppliers devoid of feeling. Perhaps a role approach would be less worrisome if birthparents were routinely held in high regard, but they are not. The status of birthparents will never move forward if we continually focus on what they can do for others rather than who they are as persons. There is room for birthparents in ongoing open adoptions for many reasons, not the least of which is the simple fact that they are numbered among God's children. Quite apart from their usefulness to others, they are important as persons.

All this raises the possibility that rather than creating and clarifying expectations of birthparents in a formal or prescriptive manner, we may be wiser to encourage birthparents, adoptive parents, and children to simply be together. Being an effective open adoption birthparent, I think, has less to do with what she is supposed to be doing than with the extent of the connection she feels to the others involved. As the years go by, I am increasingly sure that open adoption is less a set of behaviors than it is an emotional and spiritual connection. Admittedly, this is a little esoteric, but I believe this view takes us closer to the heart of open adoption than does a role perspective. One could, I suppose, mechanically fill the role of birthparent if it existed, but I do not think one can be an effective birthparent in open adoption in a mechanical fashion. Better to have interpersonal connection without a script than a script without connection. The hazard in pursuing a role-focused understanding of the birthparent experience in open adoption is that it distracts us from the simple fact that open adoption is, in most basic terms, a relationship.

I sometimes wonder if our determination to find an adequate description of the role of birthparents does not betray our worry about the capacity or willingness of participants to establish meaningful relationships. Perhaps we are interested in clearly delineated roles because we expect that filling them will spare us the work of building meaningful relationships. Experience suggests that participants do not very often "fall into" effective open adoptions. Instead, they work at them and bring them to life with loving effort. As helpful as clarity is, it's no substitute for authentic caring for others.

I can hear the grail-seekers howling. "Too vague! What's this 'connection' business, anyway? What does it look like? How does it work? Back to the ancient books! Look under that rock over there! We have to find some instructions. We have to be able to tell people what they're supposed to do, or they'll go in circles. We need the formula!"

Factors that Give Shape to the Arrangement

Is the birthparent circumstance as formless as birthparents presume? I think not. We have plenty of ideas to work with that give shape and substance to the birthparent experience without formalizing a role. We have a working definition of open adoption, a unique sense of purpose that each birthparent brings to the process, a beginning description of basic status or function, a negotiated plan, overarching values to guide the interaction, a set of responsibilities to uphold, a sense of etiquette, a variety of common interests to pursue and, eventually, established routines and traditions to uphold. None of these are small items; we have plenty of tools to bring to bear on the question of how birth-parents fit in. Quite possibly all we lack is a precise script for standard behavior, and, as we have discussed, that may be just as well.

Let's head for the shed and examine some of these tools. Many in number, they offer a versatility in approaching open adoption relationships that is not available in the one-size-fits-all approach of a formal, scripted role.

Definition. Open adoption can be defined as a legal transfer of parental rights from one family to another in a way that encourages a continuing relationship between the child and his or her birthfamily. This definition points us in a promising direction. When the participants enter into adoption on an open basis, they are expressing both the belief that children benefit from ongoing contact with their birthfamilies, and their earnest intention to nurture this uniquely meaningful relationship.

Purpose. Each birthparent who chooses open adoption has a purpose in mind—typically to advance her child's prospects for stability and opportunity—and this purpose gives shape to the process she fashions and the relationships she sets into motion. Obviously, if we are to rely on the stated purpose of an adoption decision to provide direction, we have to formulate that purpose clearly.

Basic function. In Chapter 9, we described birthparents as lifegivers, and adoptive parents as caregivers. This characterization of their routes to parenthood gives birthparents and adoptive parents a basic sense of what each is about and how they are interdependent.

The plan. Each well-designed open adoption is based on a basic plan on which the participants negotiate and agree. This initial plan sets a pattern that is fine-tuned over time.

Values. As important as plans are, not even the most carefully constructed plan can anticipate the unimaginable twists and turns that lie ahead. Consequently, agreement about the values that underlie the arrangement is important. Although we often think of values as fuzzy ideals that lurk vaguely in the background, they can bring great clarity to situations that might otherwise be confusing. Certainly this is true of open adoption's two most crucial values, candor and the resolve to honor the child in all that is done. When participants are committed to candor, for example, they know they must bring a spirit of honesty and kindness to their interactions. Hopefully, the determination to honor the child is of paramount importance to all of the adults involved. As the child matures and grows in her ability to express her needs and wishes, she brings a new set of possibilities to the circumstance.

Responsibilities. When the focus of planning is on the comfort of the adults involved in the adoption, the discussion is about options and possibilities. When the focus is on the child, expectations come into sharper focus and the talk is less vague or evasive. As participants grow in their resolve that open adoption must genuinely serve the child, they increasingly find themselves using the language of responsibility. The birthparent has a responsibility to respond to her child's questions about the adoption and all that went into it. In doing this, she affirms the child's importance and demonstrates her never-ending love. She has a responsibility to provide the adoptive family with updated medical information and to keep the family aware of her location so communication can be swift in the event an urgent situation arises. Adoptive parents, of course, have reciprocal responsibilities, which we will explore in Chapter 13.

Etiquette. Courtesy is a star that guides successful relationships in every sphere of life. This is especially true in the early stages of relationship building when things seem a bit contrived and when there is not much history to draw upon. Etiquette calls the participants in an open adoption to be sensitive to the feelings of the other parties involved. It is particularly important that everyone allow for the feelings of the other children who are involved with the families. Courtesy sets the stage for reciprocity and cooperation.

Common interests. In choosing the most promising persons to take on the responsibilities of everyday caregiving, birthparents usually select adoptive parents with whom they share a variety of interests. These interests are the common bond that brings them together, and it makes sense that they spend time exploring them. If they share an interest in old bookstores, for example, they do well to spend some time poking through a few of these dusty treasures. Open adoptions are most satisfying when they get out of the house and enter the mainstream of life.

Routines and traditions. Participants learn from trial and error the sort of interaction that everyone finds rewarding and the sort of interaction that feels awkward. The first few years of an open adoption are especially important because, with the passage of time, relationships often settle into predictable patterns and rhythms. As is true of most relationships, the contact between birth and adoptive families will reflect the interests and activities associated with the various seasons. Families and friends make special efforts to get together during the holiday season in December, for example, so it's no surprise that open adoption families are very mindful of each other at this time. With competing demands on everyone's time at this time of the year, developing some standing holiday routines is very useful. Once these routines are established, the interactive pattern of the open adoption relationship becomes more predictable, settled, and comfortable.

"Entering the Mess"

The many shaping factors we have considered are of great assistance in organizing open adoption relationships. As helpful as these factors are, however, a measure of mystery about these remarkable relationships will endure. These unknowable, intangible dimensions are responsible for much of the anxiety of open adoption, but they also account for the delight of the arrangements. Whenever we launch a new relationship, we step into promising but slightly anxious realm of unforeseeable possibilities.

I remember an interesting moment at Catholic Human Services' sixth national conference on open adoption. The finest thinkers in the field were on hand, and we were discussing the ways in which siblings—birth and adoptive—are affected by open adoption. We considered this difficult matter from a number of angles and soon found ourselves overwhelmed. It was a struggle to find terms that were even remotely adequate for the diverse and consequential relationships we were considering, and we were appropriately humbled. For all the brain power assembled, the most astute observation to come out of the discussion was, "It's a mess."

I had hoped for a little more. The conclusion, "It's a mess," did not strike me as especially enlightening, sophisticated, scientific, or dignified. I must admit, however, that the notion has grown on me over time. It might not be a very pretty description of what goes on, but, for all its homeliness, the word holds a lot of truth. It is the nature of open adoption, I think, to be a little on the messy side. And just as the word makes surprising sense for sibling issues, it makes sense for our consideration of how birthparents fit into ongoing open adoptions.

This unglamorous talk of messes is not as discouraging as it sounds. Consider another of Eugene Peterson's insights. In *Under the Unpredictable Plant: An Exploration in Vocational Holiness* [1992], commenting on the challenge of interacting with his all too human congregation, he confesses,

> I hate the mess. I hate the uncertainty. I hate not knowing how long this is going to last, hate the unanswered questions, the limbo of confused and indecisive lives, the tangle of motives and emotions. What I love is the creativity. And what I know is

that I can never be involved in creativity except by entering the mess. Mess is the precondition of creativity.... In any creative enterprise there are risks, mistakes, false starts, failures, frustrations, embarrassments, but out of this mess—when we stay with it long enough—there slowly emerges love or beauty or peace [pp.163–164].

We can bemoan the lack of a precise script, or we can roll up our sleeves and enjoy the creative challenge of finding ways to meaningfully connect to the people in our lives. Relationships may be a little messy, but they are also an important gateway to love and beauty and peace.

Factors that Give Shape to the Relationship

We may struggle in our thinking about roles, but most of us are very much at home in the realm of relationships. For all their complexity, relationships are familiar to us, and each of us has a number of thoughts about matters that enhance or detract from them. Let's highlight a handful of factors that guide birthparents in their interactions and give shape to open adoption relationships.

Goodwill. Participants in open adoptions must view each other with goodwill: It is vital. This means they take a positive view of each other and give each other the benefit of the doubt. It also means they are inclined to forgive each other's shortcomings. Cooperation flows naturally out of an atmosphere of goodwill.

Honesty. Wise birthparents and adoptive parents pledge that they will be truthful with each other. If they are sincere about this pledge, each feels obligated to put their cards on the table and let the other know where they truthfully stand on issues that arise. As long as this commitment to honesty is teamed with kindness, it will serve them well.

Humor. Since open adoption involves a number of heavy themes—loss, fear, shame, and regret, to mention a few—humor is of inestimable value as a remedy to the emotional heaviness. A sense of humor helps relieve moments of tension and keeps things in perspective. If participants can laugh at their mistakes, the relationship can be fun.

Boundaries. By staking out the limits of what is possible, clear boundaries contribute to strong relationships. A spirit of candor facilitates the process of interpersonal sharing, but it does not require that anyone forfeit his or her right to reasonable privacy. As is true in other relationships, the parties involved do well to steer clear of sex, religion, and politics.

Sense of partnership. Birthparents and adoptive parents in open adoptions are in it together for the long haul. They are aware of their interdependence, are comfortable with it, and, in the best of situations, learn to enjoy it. They appreciate each other's importance and are appropriately protective of the other's interests. They help each other look good.

Openness. It only makes sense that open adoption relationships feature an attitude of openness. Truly effective participants face the many unknowns of the future with a spirit of adventure and look to the future with a sense of wonder.

Open Adoption as an Adventure

So open adoption appears to have no Holy Grail—there is no official script for appropriate birthparent behavior. The next birthparent to come along cannot safely presume that her experience will closely resemble that of her predecessors. She may find their descriptions of their journeys informative, but that is all their accounts can be for her. Her journey will very likely hold important similarities to the travels of those who have gone before her, but we can be sure it will be a very distinct experience. How can it be otherwise? She is a very different person, and she will trek through different territories with different companions at a different point in time. A sense of role, no matter how clear or well-developed, could never prepare her for all that awaits her. Properly understood, she is stepping into the adventure of an emerging relationship. The glory of open adoption is that every relationship is uniquely created by the people who live it out. That glory more than compensates for the missing grail.

Chapter 11

Reluctant Birthparents: Foot-Dragging in the Realm of Opportunity

Some birthparents who are considering adoption are not drawn to genuine open adoption. They like the idea of choosing the adoptive family and meeting them, but, for some, that is as far as they are inclined to go. This realization came as a great surprise to me. In our early years, Catholic Human Services had one of only a handful of programs nationwide offering open adoption. Since our approach was unique, we were approached by potential birthparents from some distance who were ecstatic to find true openness. It seemed that every birthparent who approached us had high hopes for extensive openness, and we presumed this enthusiastic embrace of ongoing involvement was the new reality in adoption.

I remember the first few times I encountered birthparents who did not see it that way. Their hesitation confused me and threw me off stride. I was accustomed to initial resistance among prospective adoptive parents about open adoption, but I did not expect it from birthparents. Where we formerly ran into nearly unanimous enthusiasm, we now find occasional reluctance. To our amazement, we are having to develop new educational skills. Just as we once had to find ways to catch the attention of adoptive parents, we are now

learning how to adequately provide birthparents with information about the advantages children enjoy when their
birthfamilies stay involved.

I am not the only one to find this reluctance puzzling.
Birthparents who either enjoy full-fledged openness or who
desperately wish they had more of it often find it difficult to
understand the hesitation of their comrades. It is also difficult for adoptive parents who are enthusiastic about open
adoption to understand foot-dragging by their children's
birthparents. It frustrates them because, convinced as they
are that birthparents are important to children, they worry
that their children will suffer from the absence of their
birthparents. Just as many birthparents feel betrayed by elusive and noncommittal adoptive parents, many adoptive
parents feel let down by birthparents who fade out of their
children's lives.

Of even greater concern is the possibility that the children may interpret their birthmothers' absence as a second
round of disengagement. They may be willing to grant that
the original adoption decision was both necessary and
loving, but how is the subsequent choice of emotional distance to be explained? In an era when open adoption is
becoming widely available, there is a good chance that birthparents who decide not to stay involved may face some extra
questions down the line: "You could have shared in my
life, but you weren't there. Where were you? Did it occur to
you that I might have a few questions along the way about
my life story? If you claim to care for me so deeply, why did
you stay away?"

The first people to squirm as they try to answer these
blunt questions will be the adoptive parents. Most are deeply
appreciative of their children's birthparents and are determined to do all they can to defend their honor. The adoptive

parents can sincerely vouch for the birthmother's love and concern in planning the adoption, but they are hard-pressed to explain and defend her absence through the subsequent years. The truth is, adoptive parents may have their own frustrations with a birthparent whom they perceive as missing in action. It exasperates them to see their child's sadness go unrelieved when they know a little bit of attention could have so much meaning. Adoptive parents' frustration is especially likely in situations where one of their children enjoys a rich and satisfying relationship with his birthclan while another goes without. Of course, since it is impossible for two open adoptions to feature identical patterns of interaction, this dynamic of unequal contact is a factor to some degree in every open adoption family who adopts more than one child.

Ultimately, however, the birthparent herself will feel the weight of the question most intensely, for a day of reckoning will surely come when she will be questioned directly about the matter. Some adoptees may respond with understanding and forgiveness, but others may not. There is a chance that, in the eyes of the adopted child, disengagement by choice will turn out to be an unforgivable sin. Foot-dragging, it turns out, is risky business.

Reasons for Reluctance

We must be careful about reaching speedy conclusions, especially negative ones, about birthparents who are reluctant to sustain contact. Many factors can explain their reticence. In some rare instances, their lack of involvement may result from disinterest; but far more often, their reluctance is actually testimony, perhaps in convoluted form, to their continuing love and concern. Let's take a closer look at some possible reasons why birthparents may choose to be uninvolved.

Continued ambivalence. In Chapter 6, we explored the ambivalence of birthparents as they wrestle with the adoption decision. For many birthparents, making and implementing the decision does not magically settle the issue. Emotionally, continued ambivalence shows itself as regret. Behaviorally, it is revealed in hesitation. Many people, when unsure of themselves, end up doing nothing.

Emotional torture. A significant number of birthparents see ongoing involvement with their children as too painful to attempt. The child exists tantalizingly just out of reach—so close and yet so far. The birthmother anticipates that personal contact will chafe the open sore of her unspeakable loss, and she cannot imagine any means to cope with these unsettling feelings adequately. This sense of emotional torment may be especially intense during the child's first couple of years, when the feelings of loss are most acute and raw. The birthparent is immobilized by grief, and the thought of interaction with the baby activates her excruciating sense of helplessness.

Fear of the child's judgment. Some birthmothers are almost afraid of their children. They fear the child's rejection. "I am so afraid he will grow up to hate me," the birthparent might say. Perhaps putting too little faith in her child's natural inclination to trust the decisions of adults, she dreads the idea of facing him and making explanations. Ironically, if her fear keeps her from maintaining contact with the child, her fear might someday be realized.

Reading the "Unwelcome" sign. Birthparents commonly enter open adoption relationships with feelings of insecurity. They are worried about rejection, and their antennae are keenly tuned to signs of uneasiness in the adoptive parents. Sometimes, their anxiety may cause them to see rejecting signals where none exist. Often, however, they are on to something when they sense hesitation in the adoptive parents. They must be careful to distinguish between real hints that they "get lost," on the one hand, and, on the other, adoptive parents' awkwardness rooted in their uncertainty about interactive routines.

Offering a presumed favor. A surprising number of birthparents simply presume that adoptive parents want to be left alone. Reluctant to intrude, they keep their distance so the adoptive family can get organized without distractions. Many birthparents are shocked to discover that adoptive parents frequently long for their continued involvement.

Fear of impulsiveness. Some birthparents stay detached and uninvolved because they do not trust their ability to manage interaction with the adoptive family in acceptable fashion. They fear they might do something "crazy" in a moment of weakness, so they defend against this possibility by keeping themselves uninformed and at arm's length.

Shame. Many birthparents cannot get beyond a haunting sense that the entire experience was a shabby chapter in their lives, and they want to keep it from public sight. Ongoing interaction with the adoptive family would undermine the birthparent's efforts to hide her shameful experience, so she keeps her distance.

Unworthiness. Some birthparents feel they have failed so miserably that they do not deserve ongoing involvement. They reason that they are so flawed that their children would not benefit from a continuing relationship. For some, detachment from the adoptive family appears to be a form of self-imposed punishment.

Unrecognized personal importance. It doesn't occur to many birthparents that they have anything important to offer their children. They buy into the out-of-date notion that a good and loving birthparent recedes into the background.

Not aware that the role of lifegiver has many important on-going dimensions, the birthmother backs off in the belief that this is in the best interest of her child.

Fear of negatively affecting the child. Some birthparents are deeply worried that their presence in the lives of their youngsters might confuse them. Although our experience with open adoption clearly shows this is not true—confusion is far more likely in the absence of information than in the presence of it—they step back from the adoptive families rather than run any risks to their children.

Distance from painful memories and relationships. For some birthparents, the child is a powerful reminder of a very difficult time in life. The decision to step back from the relationship is rooted in the birthparent's desire to move beyond a devastating relationship or traumatic memories from the past.

Simplicity and closure. Some birthparents are overwhelmed by circumstances; others simply wish to move on. The birthmother may believe that an ongoing relationship with the child and adoptive family entails responsibilities and obligations that could interfere with other important activities and goals she is pursuing. She concludes that she doesn't have the energy or resources to continue this complicated relationship.

Total satisfaction with the arrangement. Some birthparents are so pleased with the way things came together at the time of placement that they feel no need to stay involved. As they see it, the adoption by loving, competent parents was mission accomplished.

Faith. For many birthparents, faith is of great importance in helping them cope with overwhelming circumstances. This was especially true in the days of closed adoption, when faith was often the only comfort available to birthparents, but it remains a significant source of strength even in this age of openness. Trusting in the competence of the system, the goodwill of adoptive parents, and God's oversight of it all, some are at peace "letting it be."

Concession to the preference of others. Many people, especially those who are not very well-informed about adoption, believe the simplest, most reliable way to get beyond a difficult life experience is to bring the curtain down and move ahead without looking back. Most birthparents will encounter such advice, and it will appeal to some. In some instances, significant others may demand a fresh start and assert great pressure toward that end.

Cynicism. Some hardened birthparents have lost faith in humankind. Unable to trust, they presume it is only a matter of time before the open adoption unravels and disappoints them. Rather than open themselves to that disappointment, they decide not to risk any involvement.

Disinterest. Sadly, some birthparents take little interest in their children. As they see it, the entire episode was a huge mistake, and they are glad to be out from under it. There is no way around the stark fact that some birthparents are only interested in themselves.

Often, the complicated dynamics that prompt birthparents to back off are felt most powerfully in the early years. This is a difficult truth, because the enduring rhythms of most open adoption relationships are established in the first couple of years. It doesn't take long for everyone to grow accustomed to absent birthparents. Even if birthparents subsequently grow beyond their initial hesitation, reestablishing contact with the adoptive family can be difficult once the continuity of interaction has been lost.

So we see a variety reasons and combinations of reasons why some birthparents choose not to stay involved with their children and the families who adopt them. Some are chilly and unimpressive, but most point convincingly to the depth of love birthparents feel for their children. The decision whether to stay involved often boils down to their thinking about the best way to deal with their incredible pain. Some birthparents believe the most promising course of pain management is to press ahead with their adoptive relationships; others conclude that the pain will subside most quickly if they step back. Either way, they face difficult challenges. No matter which course they choose, their pain is indisputable evidence of their deep love for their children.

Addressing the Concerns

The fears and hurts that inhibit birthparent involvement are numerous and complex. Their concerns take many forms and exhibit many degrees of intensity. To some extent, all birthparents have such worries. Even highly effective birthparents who enjoy mature and deeply satisfying open adoption relationships experience occasional moments of hesitation. Small wonder, then, that less-confident birthparents feel they are not up to the project. Overwhelmed by a succession of depleting decisions and events, the idea of finding the energy necessary for a successful open adoption relationship seems a bridge too far for a surprising number of lifegivers. Can we do anything to relieve their worries? How can we make open adoption less intimidating?

First, we must make participation in open adoptions feel safe, welcoming, and normal. Instead of treating ongoing involvement as exceptional or exotic, we should look upon this approach as the most natural and normal way to proceed. Professionals set the tone for adoption; our expectations make a great difference. Eager for direction in the face of confusing circumstances, participants routinely rise to our assumption that the birth and adoptive families will stay in touch. This calm, matter-of-fact approach to continuing involvement is encouraging for all birth and adoptive parents, but it is especially crucial for timid or insecure birthparents. Adoptive parents also play an important part in keeping birthparents engaged by making sure they feel truly welcome. It helps when the adoptive parents take the initiative and sincerely invite the birthparent to join in celebrations of various milestones in the youngster's life.

Second, since emotional pain is apparently the most powerful impediment to ongoing involvement, it's vital that we support birthparents in their grief. We must help them understand that continuing contact with the adoptive family, though painful in many ways, can help them recover from their loss and grief. Still, no matter how much support she receives, it takes courage for the birthparent to stay involved. Even in the warmest of relationships, there will be times when interaction with the youngster and the adoptive family intensifies her feelings of ambivalence, loss, and guilt. For birthparents, getting involved in an open adoption is a little like climbing back on the proverbial horse that threw them. Courage may be a promising way of dealing with bucking horses and lurching adoptions, but it is also understandably terrifying.

We also need to grow in our ability to describe the ways in which lifegivers fit into adoptive families so birthparents have a clear sense of what and how much is asked of them. When their involvement looms as a shapeless mass of obscure expectations, it isn't very appealing. They stand little chance of successfully meeting their obligations if they are unsure of what is expected of them. When they feel confident they know what they are doing, they feel much less anxious. Very importantly, they worry far less that their continuing involvement will confuse their children.

Finally, we can draw attention to the fact that, even though the intricacies of open adoption can be initially frightening, most birthparents who reach deep and discover the courage to live it out find their involvement enormously rewarding. There is great joy in continuing the relationship with the child, delight that is not available when contact is lost. The connection between birthparents and adoptive parents can be very satisfying in its own right, as well. It's not uncommon for them to become friends. Within some basic limits, continuing involvement permits birthparents to salvage a difficult life experience by reducing their losses and maximizing their gains.

Do Birthparents Have Continuing Obligations?

Not to sound hard-hearted, but I believe one can make a strong case that participation in open adoption relationships is not just a matter of birthparent comfort and preference. Having witnessed the benefits of open adoption for nearly two decades, I have come to view continuing involvement as more of an obligation than an option. I grow weary of hearing professionals encourage birthparents to "do whatever you are comfortable doing." Where do children fit into that line of thought? When did adoption become a matter of keeping adults comfortable? If we are serious about honoring children, we cannot sit back in the guise of professional objectivity and idly watch as a child's original family fades from reach.

What do we owe to the life we bring to this planet? Obviously, this is a vital question for birthparents. Different people will answer in different ways, but several thoughts occur to me. The most basic obligation of the lifegiver is to be sure her child is in a safe, nurturing environment. A carefully crafted open adoption can fully satisfy that responsibility. Some birthparents might argue that meeting this funda-

mental obligation with a secure adoptive arrangement satis-
fies all of their responsibilities, but that is debatable.

Owe is a strong word, and some may wish to quibble
over it. Admittedly, it is the sort of word that might arouse
guilt or anger for those who hold a different view. That is not
my intent in exploring the issue. Birthparents who are feeling
overwhelmed by circumstances need understanding, not
judgment. Nevertheless, even as we compassionately reach
out to birthparents who are doing the best they can in severe
circumstances, we must stand tall for the sake of the children. If we truly believe that birthfamilies have importance
in the lives of adopted children, we cannot lightly give up on
the prospect of birthparent involvement. The interests of
birthparents and children need some balancing, but whatever
we do let's forever be sure that we do not shortchange the
children. With the rights and opportunities afforded by open
adoption come responsibilities.

I am convinced there is much that lifegivers can do to
enhance their children's life circumstances beyond providing
a stable, loving family. The benefits attached to their continuing involvement are so significant that I am inclined to use
the language of obligation and responsibility. What are
these obligations?

I believe the birthparent owes her child explanations of
the reasons for the adoption decision. I say *explanations,*
plural, because this is not usually a singular event. The youngster will likely return to the subject intermittently and press
for more details as he or she grows older. Another round
of information birthparents owe their children is a vivid
accounting of the child's birth story. Everybody deserves to
know what it was like when time stood still and he or she
first entered the world.

Next, I believe children have a right to know their genealogical context. They deserve to know their place in the

intergenerational flow of life. And who can argue against the idea that children are entitled to updated medical information? There is great value in the birthparent remaining involved with the adoptive family so questions can be answered as they emerge over time. For those of us who have seen anxiety and terror in the eyes of adoptees and birthparents as they begin their search for each other after decades of disengagement, this approach clearly offers another great bonus. If the birthparent stays involved in the child's life, there is no need for him to undergo a stressful search for his roots when he is an adult.

Finally, too many adopted children struggle with feelings of rejection. It's not unreasonable to hope that lifegivers will do all they can to help their children resolve this hurtful issue. In my view, lifegivers owe their children never-ending interest and well-wishing.

We need to alert birthparents to the idea that they have continuing responsibilities and support them in their efforts to meet these obligations. Many are delighted to embrace these expectations—every step they take is guided by their determination to meet their children's needs—but others are surprised by the idea that their children continue to need them. It never occurred to them—or many other people, for that matter—that they had anything important to offer over time. Some are so drained by the pregnancy and adoption planning that they are unable to use their imaginations to see the experience through the eyes of the child. Often, the notion that they have a continuing role to play hits them as a revelation. Although the language of obligation sounds onerous at first, many birthparents grow to welcome these responsibilities once they understand them. Paradoxically, the obligation frees them to enjoy many unanticipated relationships.

Persistence and Patience

What if problem solving, reassurance, and education have little impact? What if, despite our best efforts, the birthparent keeps her distance from the adoptive family?

If the birthmother resolves that the only safe course is to lay low, we have little choice but to accept her decision. Because this decision has a potentially very serious downside, however, we must at minimum provide her the opportunity to fully explain her disengagement in writing or, better yet, on video tape. Perhaps, in some situations, if ongoing personal contact is too much for her, she can manage less intense forms of involvement, like sending letters and birthday gifts. These tangible remembrances may offer the child at least some reassuring evidence that she has not been forgotten.

Wonderfully, birth grandparents often fill the gap. They are open adoption's unsung heroes. Although they have their own adoption-related sadness, it is usually more manageable for them. In truly open adoption, grandparents, by birth or by adoption, are grandparents—how they come by the status is not relevant. Their continuing involvement with the child is very meaningful in its own right, but it also preserves the link between the two families, leaving the door open for the birthparent to reenter the situation after she has caught her emotional breath.

Even when the birthparent is determined not to be involved, hope for the future remains. We know that, whether or not she expresses interest in the child, he will remain forever on her mind. That fact raises hope that her perception and behavior may change. Time helps heal the pain. Time also brings greater maturity, a quality that may mean less dependence on others who may have discouraged contact in the early going. There is hope, too, that the persistent good-will and availability of the adoptive parents will pay off. As one undaunted adoptive mother put it, "She can't resist us forever—we're too much fun for that." And who can resist the innocent queries of a youngster wondering "Are you out there? Are you okay? Do you remember me?" When our best shot at persuasion falls short, hope for the future may be the only comfort we can muster.

Encouraging Involvement Without Judgment

So what are we to make of birthparents who drag their feet in the realm of opportunity? Two divergent impressions emerge from this discussion. On the one hand, these hurting, reluctant birthparents need and deserve our understanding. On the other, the children reap important benefits when lifegivers stay positively connected to the adoptive families. In starker terms, the total disengagement of birthparents seldom serves the best interests of children. It is wrong for us to be neutral on this matter—our first responsibility is to honor the children—but it is also wrong for us to overlook the pain of birthparents.

We must find some relief for this tension, or open adoption proponents will unwittingly create two categories of birthparents. To the horror of those of us who want to create a more respectful environment for birthparents, we will set into motion a system in which there are "good" birthparents, who remain involved with their children, and "bad" birthparents, who do not. How ironic if this movement, which set out to make life better for birthparents, ends up making things worse for many of them.

Although the situation is complicated, one thing is clear: Our approach must be respectful and positive. We must be very careful that, in helping hesitant birthparents get beyond feelings of discomfort and unworthiness, our efforts do not inadvertently generate new waves of despair. Careless intimations that they are willfully failing their children will only add to their anguish. Criticism will not relieve their reluctance; it will only drive wounded birthparents deeper into their distancing defenses. Their pain already consumes and constricts them—shall we add to it our judgment?

Far better that we approach with affirmation, encouragement, and understanding. Better that we educate and support. Better that we respectfully tap into their love for their children than to raise doubt about it. We must frame the discussion in fair-minded fashion. Properly understood, the question is never about whether birthparents love their children, it's about the best ways for them to express that love.

Chapter 12

When the Adoption Dust Settles: Optimal Birthparenting

In the early years of our open adoption practice, we were not brokenhearted when birthparents faded into the sunset after hanging around for a couple of years. These days we are. Now that we realize how meaningful it can be to the children to have ongoing relationships with their birthfamilies, we feel very defeated when birthparents fade out of the adoptions they have arranged.

This is a significant shift in the way we see things, and it raises an important issue: If we don't want birthparents to gradually disappear, what are we hoping for? When the adoption dust settles, what hopes and expectations do we have for birthparents? What is optimal birthparenting?

Before we get too far into this discussion, we should consider some of the difficulties associated with this word, *optimal*. It is an elusive concept that is easily misunderstood. How do we capture the nature of an optimal relationship when the very thing that makes it optimal is its adaptability? And there is no way around the fact that any description of optimal birthparenting will have a subjective flavor about it, since observers will hold very different ideas about what is desirable. What's more, optimal will vary according to the unique desires, capabilities, and personalities of the parties involved. An outcome that might be optimal in one situation might be undesirable in another. We must be careful not to generalize too broadly as we explore the concept of optimal birthparenting.

Another problem that comes with a discussion of optimal outcomes for birthparents is its potential to discourage those conscientious lifegivers who are doing the best they can in circumstances that are far from ideal. Sometimes, just getting through the messy necessities of the next half hour is all a person can do. Emotionally drained people are not always happy to hear glib talk about optimal outcomes.

Still another hazard with a discussion of ideals is that they can be interpreted as a set of expectations. If birthparents operate with the impression that they are supposed to be ideal or perfect in their adoptive relationships, they are certain to feel that they have fallen short and failed. No one can feel successful held to impossible standards.

My intention, then, is to identify ideals that are worth aspiring to without creating burdensome expectations. The distinction between aspirations and expectations is well worth making. Hopefully, a beginning description of ideal outcomes can provide the comfort that comes with a clear sense of direction.

When the whirlwind of activity surrounding the placement finally calms and birthparents settle in for the long haul, I believe we can look to the future with four basic goals in mind. Experience has taught us to encourage birthparents to

- recover from their losses,
- move forward toward fulfilling their lifelong goals and dreams,
- persevere in their open adoption relationships, and
- enjoy personal transformation.

These are not insignificant goals. The most fundamental is that birthparents will successfully recover from the trauma of the experience. Everything begins with this goal, for little else will be accomplished if healing does not occur. In terms of their ongoing involvement with their children and the adoptive families, we hope birthparents will somehow find a way to both move forward with their lives and "hang in there" with their children and with the adoptive families. Properly understood, these are not contradictory intentions. Finally, our most optimistic aspiration for birthparents is that they will come out of the experience positively transformed and possessing a renewed zest for life.

Recovery and Healing

Amazing as it now seems, only a generation ago was denial promoted as the best way for birthparents to handle their experience. The exit advice they received was some version of, "Just forget you ever had a baby and get on with your life. Good luck." Denial, obviously, is not recovery. Pretending something did not happen does not make it go away. One wonders how such flawed advice could hold sway as long as it did. If birthparents are to heal from their world-turned-inside-out hurt, there is work to be done.

The most obvious task of recovery is to move forward with the grieving process. The temptation to stonewall the experience and claim everything is wonderful is so formidable that we dare not presume that healthy grieving will automatically happen. The truth is, birthparents hardly know what to do with themselves early on. Hormones flare, empty arms ache, and their world drains of color. If they immerse themselves in endless reminders of loss, they can feel overwhelmed. In that state of mind, they worry that they will never shake the powerful feeling of primal loss. On the other hand, if birthparents try to act as though nothing of significance has happened, they face the horror of self-deceit and the insidious onset of emotional numbness.

The sensible course for them is to tackle the loss at a manageable pace. Grieving requires birthparents to identify their losses and fully acknowledge them. Gradually, at their own pace, they work through the various phases of grief and tackle the aspects of grieving that are unique to the their experiences as birthparents (see Chapter 7) and that are unique to them as individuals. This is a tall order, and the time it takes is measured in years, not weeks or months. Their grieving is, of course, never entirely resolved, but hopefully they find some eventual measure of peace of mind and heart.

Beyond grieving, there is invariably some damage control and repair to accomplish. The adoption choice was necessitated by momentous factors that can stagger a birthparent and leave her feeling utterly defeated. She never dreamed her life would take such a turn, and her frustration is often soul-deep. The experience may leave her feeling small and powerless; it would be easy for her to dwell on the indignity of it all and nurture the hurt. She can gradually overcome the sense of defeat, however, if she can come to fully own her portion of the decision. Most likely, the adoption plan emerged from an intricate mixture of submission and action—from surrender to factors that were beyond her control, but also from deliberate and careful decisions she made along the way. This decisive dimension is important, for an intellectual and emotional shift from passive surrender to active, loving entrustment can make a great difference in a birthparent's ability to meet life head on. It can be the difference between life as a victim and life as a participant in satisfying relationships.

Many birthparents come out of their entrustment experience with some frayed interpersonal edges. Chances are strong that many relationships were rearranged by the rigors of the adoption journey. Some relationships grew stronger, but others were fractured. Effective birthparents will do their best to address these strained and broken relationships. The hurt is deep and requires substantial courage and energy to address. The task of repair can seem futile. She thinks, "What's the use? The bum has never shown an ounce of interest in me or the baby." Or, "There's no hope. Mother is completely unwilling to talk about this." As daunting as the project appears, it's worth the effort, for it can produce meaningful understandings. On the other hand, resentment left unaddressed and unrelieved can extract a great toll through the years. Sometimes, no matter how diligent the effort to work things out, reconciliation is not possible. In those instances, it's still worthwhile for the birthparent to unilaterally move toward forgiveness so she can release any bitterness she might be holding.

An important aspect of healing is learning to hold one's head high in the face of criticism, be it her own or that of others. If a birthparent is to emerge from the experience with her sense of self-worth intact, she needs to fully settle the fundamental morality of her decision. If the decision or some aspect of it was somehow ethically off base, she needs to seek forgiveness for the mistakes she made. On the other hand, if her decisions were well-motivated and child-honoring, she has every reason to move ahead with a clear conscience. If she knows in her heart of hearts that her adoption decision was predominantly an act of love, she can hopefully enter new social circumstances feeling fully entitled to the same respectful treatment that everybody else deserves.

Moving Forward

Although she does not disappear into the sunset, an effective birthparent surely does move forward with her life.

Neither in denial about her adoption experience nor pre-occupied with it, she has perspective and balance. Her on-going responsibilities as a birthparent are very important to her, but they do not dominate her existence. It is, hope-fully, but one satisfying set of relationships among many in her life. Ideally, she is neither underinvested nor over-invested in the task of carrying out her ongoing adoption responsibilities.

Clear-headedness about the fundamentals of the arrangement makes it possible for birthparents to move forward. To the extent she is clear about the distinction between caregivers and lifegivers, the birthparent will understand and remember she has totally transferred the daily responsibilities of parenting to other capable hands. While this transfer does not for a moment mean that her caring stops, it does mean that she can let go of the day in, day out worrying that goes with hands-on parenting. Fortunately, the regular contact afforded by open adoption has the advantage of reassuring birthparents how capable those other hands really are. Knowing from personal observation that all is well with the youngster and that the adoptive family would notify her if something serious was happening enables the birthmother to turn her emotional energy in other directions.

We are talking about trust. In many ways, the ability of birthparents to move forward in life depends on their ability to fully trust the adoptive parents. When trust runs high, it is much easier for a birthmother to let go of her worries. On the other hand, it is very difficult to move forward when trust is limited. Trust cannot be manipulated or rushed; it grows with time and with consistency. It is of paramount importance in open adoption relationships, and all the participants must do their best to nurture it.

Truly effective birthparents have a forward outlook. They look to the future with confidence and excitement. Although the open adoption decision is emotionally exhausting, it does spare birthparents the energy-draining rigors of active-duty parenting and affords them the chance to apply themselves toward accomplishing life goals. Sadly, the pressing duties of daily parenting may derail the dreams of some of their peers who chose to raise their children as single parents. The forward leaning birthparent, hopefully, is positioned to continue her march toward realizing her potential and achieving her longstanding goals. Things do not automatically work out this way, but the adoption decision does hold this potential.

Birthparents sometimes feel guilty about the renewed personal opportunity they experience because of their adoption decisions. Given the superhuman expectations that swirl around motherhood, they often feel they were supposed to be entirely selfless in their decisions about the future and that their own hopes and dreams are unimportant. This guilt is misguided for a couple of reasons. First, there is room in the decision-making process for reasonable and appropriate self-interest. Second, and just as importantly, a birthparent's ability to move ahead in life is great news for her child. Although adopted children often do take heart in learning about the anguish of the adoption decision, they are far better served by the effectiveness of their birthparents than by their birthparents' impairment. The birthparent's life apart from adoption enriches the child's life as it brings him the prospect of extra stimulation and extra opportunity. The effectiveness of his birthparent becomes a source of pride for the child and positively affects his self-concept.

Hanging In There

Not only do effective birthparents move forward in life, they also stay meaningfully involved with their children and the adoptive families. In thinking about birthparent involvement, most people immediately focus on the rate of interaction. As significant as frequency of contact is, its importance can be overstated. Infrequent interaction does not automatically mean dissatisfaction, and frequent contact does not guarantee contentment. More important to optimal birthparenting than frequent contact is the quality of the contact. Wording it a little differently, successful open adoption is better understood in terms of forming warm and fulfilling relationships than with frequency of contact. A birthparent's satisfaction with adoption is directly related to the quality of the relationships she enters.

Throughout this book, we have seen that ambivalence is a major theme for birthparents. The circumstances leading to pregnancy and adoption are seldom clear-cut and simple, so mixed or contradictory feelings are common. About the beauty and wonder of the child, however, there is no ambivalence. An effective lifegiver wholeheartedly and unambivalently affirms, honors, and delights in her child's existence, and this reveling spirit is great news for the adopted child. What, after all, might the converse mean to a child? What does it mean to a child to know that she is the source of humiliation and shame to her birthparents? Obviously, it is far more pleasing for a child to consider herself a source of delight to the vital people in her life than to think of herself as an accident or an embarrassment.

The child's well-being is the essential issue for affirming lifegivers, the absolute heart of the matter. The birthmother may have many hopes and dreams for the open adoption, but her priority is that her child is positioned and equipped for a full and satisfying life. This priority is very consequential. It means the birthparent puts substantial energy into building and nourishing her relationship with the child. And it means she is at least intuitively aware of his developmental stages and what they mean for her relationship with him. Above all, it means she realizes the importance of keeping her contact with him consistent and dependable. Because this relationship is extremely important to her, she is willing to be personally inconvenienced if necessary so the relationship can be advanced.

Although she does not carry the emotional presence of an everyday parent, an involved birthparent is much more than a memory, myth, or merrymaker. She is a lifegiver, and as such has much to offer to her child. Ideally, she will carry out the ongoing duties of a lifegiver with diplomacy, competence, and good humor. Rather than looming as a rival caregiver, she supports the adoptive parents in their parental capacity. Without overdoing it, she encourages and endorses the adoptive parents as they work through the humbling challenges of parenthood. As a friend of the family—far from a competitor or alternate parent—she makes it clear that she is not there to criticize their child care techniques. Fully committed to teamwork, an effective birthparent does not take unilateral action; she has an interactive, collaborative style. If the adoptive parents are fair-minded, it usually doesn't take long for them to welcome her as a true member of the extended family.

A birthparent with at least a beginning sense of how she fits into the picture is free to enjoy her relationships with the child and with the adoptive parents. In the context of great loss and sadness, *enjoy* is admittedly quite a word. Its use is not meant to deny the pain of the total circumstance or the extraordinary effort that goes into building relationships. Nevertheless, an effective birthparent does ultimately find her adoptive relationships satisfying. Through a mixture of intuition, asking questions, and a sometimes awkward process of trial and error, she gradually figures out the routines of the adoptive family and how she fits into them. Once she feels connected to the various members of the family, she can relax and settle in.

Quality adoption relationships obviously require nurturing. Although she is eager to establish a lasting connection, a wise lifegiver is patient because building worthwhile relationships takes time. We know in advance there will be disappointments. If a birthparent is to find lasting comfort in the arrangement, she must come to terms with the downside of the experience—the imperfection of adoptive parents, the rudeness of outsiders, and her own intermittent feelings of envy. She will need stamina to weather the times of doubt and to adjust to the unpredictable twists and turns the adoption will take. It is an endless learning process, for no one ever masters the open adoption experience. Just when a comfortable rhythm is discovered, the child moves into a new stage of development that calls for a new set of responses from both the adoptive parents and the birthparent. It helps if she enjoys learning.

One person on her own cannot make a relationship work, but an effective birthparent does everything she can to hold up her end of the relationship. Since our most satisfying relationships are multidimensional, a savvy lifegiver finds ways to move the interaction beyond polite living room conversation and into the mainstream of everyday life. Open adoption relationships are at their best at football games, on the garage sale circuit, or in the sanctuary. As participants explore mutual interests and share diverse experiences, the lifegiver becomes a welcome and trusted friend of the adoptive family. If active friendship is for some reason out of reach—friendships, of course, cannot be forced—at least she does all she can keep things amicable.

A birthparent who is functioning in optimal form attends to the little things that make such a difference, and she is attentive to the etiquette of open adoption. Open adoption etiquette, it turns out, is not much different from the basic courtesy that applies to any friendly relationship. When it is time to visit, she communicates her plans clearly and well in advance. If she is running late, she calls to let folks know. She remembers Mother's Day (and hopefully is remembered) with a card or a phone call. In the fashion of a wise mother-in-law, she knows when to keep her opinions—especially about parenting—to herself unless asked for her ideas. A thoughtful birthparent is also very sensitive to the needs of other children in the adoptive family and goes out of her way to cultivate feelings of kinship with them.

Over time, as the lifegiver finds a comfortable place in the family configuration, her interaction with the family becomes routine. Gradually, her consistency and goodwill take root, and she assumes the oddly wonderful status of being taken for granted. Less fuss is made over her, and, in the paradoxical fashion of routine family life, her lack of special status means she has arrived as a valued member of the family. No longer a guest, she is family. Hopefully, this experience of joining a family works both ways. Just as the lifegiver gradually enters the circle of the adoptive family, they join hers. In the best situations, each family gains new members. Chapter 13 describes several ways in which adoptive parents can help birthparents to fit in.

Most of the optimal birthparenting I have been describing presumes receptive adoptive parents. Obviously, that is not always the case. Some of the most impressive birthparents I have met do not enjoy the blessing of reciprocal relationships. In spite of covert or overt resistance from adoptive parents, they work with amazing creativity and energy to maintain a constructive link with the families. Remarkably, they somehow find ways to manage their frustrations and keep their connections to their children vital and constructive. Although there are many limits to what they can accomplish, these too are optimal birthparents. To their great credit, they are doing everything they reasonably can to assure the children of their love.

Transformation

Embedded in the crisis and pain of the adoption experience is the prospect for extraordinary personal growth. Contemporary birthparenting is potentially very different from the devastating days when birthparents were routinely flattened by a hit-and-run truck called secrecy. These days, it is more possible than ever before for birthparents to come out of the experience positively transformed.

A fully open birthparent knows the comfort of candor. She is honest with herself and with the people in her life who matter. Although it might be tempting for her to keep some relatives and friends in the dark, she rises above that temptation and lets the truth of her circumstance be known. As a result, she is not burdened with the consuming task of maintaining secrets. An effective lifegiver knows the wonderful liberation that comes with being established as an imperfect person. While people around her may struggle mightily to defend their images, she has little need for pretense. Although she once feared that she would be unacceptable to others if they knew her imperfections, she finds that her authenticity more often attracts the confidence of others. Comfortably imperfect, she can laugh at the little shortcomings of life and disarm them. She knows that a sense of humor is crucial to the formation of satisfying open adoption relationships.

Transformed birthparents invariably have great compassion for the hard times of others. They are gentle in their handling of others and slow to judge because they know firsthand the sting of community disapproval. They know from experience how complicated things can be and that fault finders seldom have all the facts. Fully aware of the healing power of understanding, most birthparents are quicker to put an arm of friendship around a wounded soul than to join the chorus of critics. Having experienced a measure of healing, they become healers.

Coming out of an open adoption experience, an affirming birthparent is wiser and more clear about her priorities. Every value she holds dear has been tested during her adoption journey, and better than most she knows the emotional cost of standing by them. Because experience has taught her the difference between major and minor issues, a transformed lifegiver is not very likely to be distracted by superficial issues. Many birthparents report that they have come out their experiences much stronger as individuals than they felt going into them.

One of the great hopes for all participants in open adoption is that the spirit of openness will generalize to other dimensions of life. If an attitude of openness improves the adoption experience, it makes sense that such openness may apply to other situations as well. If the openness of the experience rubs off on her and becomes her preferred way to tackle new situations, chances are strong that she will meet with many satisfying results in a wide range of circumstances.

Although birthparents often enter their adoption experiences with a great sense of loneliness, hopefully they come to know that they are part of a supportive and unusually gracious community. The chance to affiliate with peers and find soul mates validates an experience that might otherwise seem completely unique and beyond the comprehension of others. An affirming birthparent has a very full life, but that does not alter the fact that she remains available to other birthparents and interested parties. Through her affiliation with peers, she both finds role models and becomes a role model for others.

As she reflects on her experiences and grows in her ability to articulate them, she joins the effort to more fully define the rightful place of lifegivers in the open adoption experience. Emboldened with the knowledge that she is not alone, an effective lifegiver will at least occasionally set aside the comfort of invisibility and share the truth of her personal experience. In doing this, she takes an important step toward improving the shadowy image of birthparents. Some will do more. Some will become actively involved in the adoption reform movement and do their best to improve the institution for those who follow.

We must be honest and recognize that effectiveness does not erase tragedy. When parents and children are separated, there is a sadness that never goes away. That is an irrefutable truth, but there is a parallel truth: Birthparents who have the courage to take on the fullness of the open adoption experience tap into the power of cooperation and faith. Through carefully placed trust and hard work, they earn the conviction that devastating situations, if approached with a spirit of love and candor, can be reworked and transformed into something extraordinary. Can we envision a better adoptive outcome than this? Is there any skill in life to match the beauty of the redemptive touch? Is there any perspective or ability we would rather model for our children than the ability to turn traumatic circumstances into triumphs?

When the adoption dust settles and heads stop spinning, our most basic hope is that birthparents will come through the journey okay. Although they may have lasting scars, we hope they largely recover from their hurts and losses. And while we hope they continue to move forward to experience the fullness of life, we also hope they are persevering and faithful in maintaining their open adoption relationships. Most audaciously, we hope it all comes together to produce the hard-earned sweetness of personal transformation. Rather than looking back on their adoption journeys as diminishing experiences, we dare to hope they will find themselves unexpectedly enriched.

Chapter 13

Welcoming Birthparents as Full-Status Participants in the Adoption Process

Although the purpose of this book is to help interested people to understand birthparents and their circumstances more fully, I expect that many birthparents who have read this far have experienced it as a call to rise up and function at a high level. Undoubtedly, many challenging suggestions have been implied as we have explored various dynamics, and some of these intimations admittedly approach the impossible.

Among other things, for example, birthparents are urged to tend faithfully to their own needs while remaining very sensitive to the needs of others. They are advised to be appropriately assertive, but also to remain patient with the foibles of the others involved. Go ahead and take the risks associated with trust, the narrative exhorts, but by all means stay heads up and wary. Learn to live with your ambivalence. And while we're at it, never miss a chance to tell your intimate stories to the crowds of critics you encounter along the way. The implied suggestions go on and on, and it may seem to birthparents that the burden for making open adoption work is placed solely at their doorstep.

To some extent, at least, my intention is to challenge birthparents to be more and do more than they have in the past. I do mean to call them to carry themselves with great dignity and effectiveness, and I do hope they will step forward and share their extraordinary insights with those who are willing to listen. Years of interacting with these loving lifegivers have left me deeply impressed with their capabilities, and I am convinced they have the potential to redesign the institution of adoption for the better. I wish to be very clear, however, that I believe the responsibility to work for constructive change is shared by everyone who cares about the past, present, and future of adoption. Birthparents own a portion of this responsibility, but everyone involved needs to join the effort to transform adoption into an institution that is more balanced and more inclusive of birthparents.

A Tilted Field

A lot of work must be done if adoption is to welcome birthparents as full-status participants. I am convinced the playing field in adoption is far from level, and—to extend the sports metaphor—the team with the fewest advantages is forever traveling uphill against the wind. Birthparents and adoptive parents are far from equals in their shared journey, and this inequality seriously detracts from the well-being of everyone involved. How can an institution generate healthy results if it regularly caters to the advantaged participants while disempowering the disadvantaged?

An uncomfortable truth in adoption is that, for several reasons, the playing field clearly tilts in favor of adoptive parents. Adoption is usually organized and carried out by members of the middle class. Most of the time, these professionals find it easier to identify with adoptive parents than with birthparents, who are typically less established. As "deserving" people who have lived upright lives but have had little luck getting pregnant, the plight of adoptive parents tugs on the heartstrings and elicits a compassionate response.

Furthermore, since adoptive parents usually underwrite the process through the fees they pay, it's hardly surprising that professionals make an extra effort to keep them satisfied. Also, most adoptive parents have a hefty measure of standing in their communities. If they are content, they can do a lot to further the interests of an adoption program. Conversely, if they are unhappy with a particular service provider, they have the clout to make things difficult.

In contrast to the confidence with which adoptive parents have approached the system through the years, birthparents frequently have found it inhospitable. Even those who feel they were treated with respect sometimes avoid the organization that handled their adoptions because the memories are so painful. Few birthparents feel much emotional investment in or ownership of the program they turned to in their time of need. Few birthparents refer to the organization they went through with the enthusiastic claim, "That's my program!" Close listeners recognize it is adoptive parents who use possessive pronouns when referring to those who guided them through the process. Most adoption programs belong to adoptive parents.

Let me quickly follow the assertion that adoptive parents are the favored parties with a couple of important clarifications. First of all, I am not saying that the process is easy for them, because it is not. Most of the time, adoptive parents enter the experience wounded by a maddening struggle with infertility and all the depletion of privacy, finances, time, and hope that goes with that condition. The fact that many adoptive parents find the adoptive process wearisome and intrusive even though it is designed to meet their needs first tells us a great deal about the insensitivity of the process. If the favored parties sometimes wonder about the ways they are treated, what does this mean for those who are less favored?

Second, I do not want to blame adoptive parents for the lack of balance in the system. They did not design the system; professionals did. Rather than disparage adoptive parents, I believe we need to salute them. I am impressed with the sensitivity of most of the adoptive parents I have come to know, and I am convinced that—with the benefit of imaginative preparation—they wholeheartedly welcome a system of adoption that is driven by concern for children and that honors birthparents. I will have more to say about this later.

Making the System More Birthparent Friendly

The idea of organizing the system so it is more inclusive of birthparents calls for a major review of the way adoption programs are organized. If we take the principle of inclusion seriously, many programs will have to significantly alter their philosophies, policies, and procedures. What can we do to serve birthparents better? What does the system owe birthparents? What will it take for us to incorporate birthparents into the process as full-status participants? This is a very different way of organizing adoption services, so we have a lot to learn about effective ways to include birthparents. New methods will emerge with experience, but several ideas are already evident.

Accessibility. A program that is genuinely concerned about birthparents is easy for them to access. Respectful, but far from stuffy, the program is approachable. Since most consumers have little familiarity with the adoption process as they begin their journey, they often assume all programs are alike. This assumption has produced many heartbreaking results as innumerable birthparents have ended up with adoptions that fall far short of their expectations. Disturbed that so many birthparents have been mislead, a conscientious program encourages its clients to stay alert and ask the hard questions. A great program finds ways to help potential consumers recognize that it is a great program.

Problem solving. Chapter 5 suggested that the birthparent journey begins with circumstances of external and internal necessity. That's where the professional response needs to begin as well. The obvious first effort is to find ways to relieve these circumstances if possible. Is the proposed adoption truly necessary? Is there a creative way to rework the situation so the family can stay intact? We ought not yield to what may prove to be transitory factors of necessity too quickly. Adoption planning does not make any sense until we have first done all we reasonably can to resolve the issues of necessity. Family preservation should come first.

"First client" status. Outstanding adoption programs are distinguished from lesser programs by the fact that they approach birthparents as their first clients. Instead of working with potential birthparents because it enables them to meet the needs of prospective adoptive parents, exemplary programs work diligently to prepare effective adoptive parents to meet the needs of prospective birthparents.

I cannot overstate the importance of this ordering. By establishing those who are grappling with untimely, awkward, or unsupported pregnancies as their primary clients, service providers take an important step to guard against the tendency to over-identify with adoptive parents. If birthparents are our first clients, it follows that we will be deeply concerned about their level of satisfaction with the process and that we will measure the success of our efforts in these terms. An outcome that leaves birthparents feeling unappreciated could never be considered a success.

Identifying with birthparents. We owe birthparents an honest effort to come alongside and identify with them. Instead of viewing birthparents as a distinctive client group with whom we have little in common, we can learn to see ourselves mirrored in them in many ways. Obviously, adoption professionals who are not birthparents cannot fully know what it is like to permanently entrust a child to the care of other parents, but we certainly can identify with the panic of being in a situation where all of the alternatives seem bleak. Surely none of us are immune from the devastation of loss, and none of us are strangers to the terror that accompanies total dependence on others. With the smallest expenditure of energy and imagination, we can see ourselves in their place and identify with their fear, their hope, and their courage.

It's unlikely we will be successful in calling adoptive parents to this sort of identification with birthparents if we cannot achieve it for ourselves. If adoption professionals can learn to enter the experience of birthparents imaginatively— to find the "birthparent within"—and view the experience of adoption through the eyes of birthparents, things will change, because it will occur to us that we would not want to be treated the way birthparents have been treated for so long.

Recognizing strengths and inviting excellence. The circumstances of the pregnancy may be awkward, untimely, or unsupported, but with rare exception the person in the circumstance is strong and capable. An expectant woman may approach the possibility of adoption feeling defeated by her circumstances, but we owe it to her to recognize her strength and tap into it. The factors that compel her to consider adoption may be overwhelming and unworkable, but the process itself should not add to her sense of defeat. Some participants simply want to get through this experience that seems so awful and get it over with, but we can do much better than this. The process is far too important for participants to muddle their way through. Professionals need to build on strengths and call their clients to greatness. We must insist on excellence, for the results we see will often match our expectations. If we truly believe in the people we are working with and for, chances are strong that they will respond.

An assumption of enduring importance to the child. In the past, birthparents were routinely treated as though they were only of short-term importance. Once they had given birth and relinquished their rights, they were presumed to have little more to offer. Decades of open adoption practice have made clear that this presumption was mistaken, for birthfamilies have much to offer as their children grow older and take greater interest in their own life stories. This realization is of great importance, for it means we cannot be neutral on the issue of birthparent involvement. Rather, we owe it to the children to actively encourage birthparents to stay involved with them. It also means we must approach birthparents with the long view in mind and strive to prepare them for the years ahead. Obviously, this is a tall order.

Equivalence. As the gap between birthparents and adoptive parents narrows, treating them similarly makes sense. If adoptive parents benefit from educational efforts, it's reasonable to expect that birthparents will too. If we sometimes need to coax birthparents to believe more fully in their capabilities, it's likely that adoptive parents will also respond positively to our encouragement. Each group needs information and reassurance. An insight that is meaningful for one group is invariably meaningful for the other. There's nothing we might say to one group that we would not feel comfortable saying to the other. As the years go by, we find

our information-gathering forms are increasingly inter-
changeable. Information worth gathering from one family is
usually worth gathering from the other.

Candor. The hallmark of open adoption is candor. If a
spirit of candor is to take hold, it must begin with the professionals involved who set the tone for all that follows. To
function with integrity, we must, as social workers, practice
what we proclaim. We owe it to birthparents to be clear
about our beliefs, procedures, and expectations. As they
work through a succession of extraordinarily significant decisions, birthparents deserve nothing less than the best information. Idealistic though it sounds, we want them to know
everything there is to know about adoption. If we embody
candor ourselves, we are positioned to invite our clients to
greater levels of candor.

Safety and empowerment. Setting an adoption in motion
is a frightening thing for a birthparent. The stakes are incom-
parably high, and the extent of the trust required defies description. Since anxiety invariably runs high, efforts to make
the process as safe as possible are of great importance.
Safety means many things in this context. It means that a
birthparent will be protected from people who pressure her
to reach particular conclusions prematurely or with little regard for her wishes. It also means she will have control over
her experience and make the crucial decisions herself. As
we have seen, it is important for professionals to call birthparents to excellence and to candor, but we must recognize
that in doing this we are intentionally setting out to influence their thinking.

In my work with birthparents, I am very conscious of the
fact that my interaction with them significantly affects the
way they experience this process. As I invite, inspire, challenge, coax, and cajole them to get beyond the constricting
immediacy of the situation and evaluate things with a view

toward the long-term effects of their decisions on the child, I recognize that, in the end, I must defer to their best thinking about these matters. I hope our discussions will be lively and informative, but I fully respect the fact that the decisions are theirs and that they must own them. This combination of deliberate challenge and ultimate deference protects them from the hazard of settling for unimaginative thinking on one hand and the disrespectful imposition of unsolicited opinions on the other.

Birthparents will also feel greater safety if they have a clear grasp of how things work and the recourse that is available to them. They have a right to written information about the adoptive process. The material to which they are entitled includes the laws that underpin the process, a detailed description of the service provider's procedures, and a clear statement of the program's grievance policy.

Skill building. Some birthparents considering adoption are blessed with the innate ability to constructively interact with prospective adoptive parents, but others are at a loss as to where to begin. An effective program will help birthparents who find it difficult to build relationships with others to develop their skills in this regard.

Grief work. Since loss is intrinsic to their experience, we know that birthparents have to grieve. Some birthparents will welcome assistance from the professional in tackling the grief involved, whereas others will prefer to look elsewhere for support. Whatever their preference, a respectful system will ensure that the dynamic of loss and grief is addressed.

Troubleshooting. Nearly every birthparent involved in an open adoption worries that something might go wrong in the relationship and shut it down. That being the case, it's a relief for birthparents to know that they can turn to the agency for assistance if the adoptive arrangement somehow gets off track. Birthparents and adoptive parents are encouraged to work things out on their own whenever possible, but an effective program remains available to all parties involved to mediate and fine tune arrangements as needed. This does not mean that things will always work out to everyone's satisfaction, but it's a comfort nevertheless to know that things can be addressed reasonably and constructively.

Program input. Programs that are serious about serving birthparents are eager to learn from them. Because they are genuinely concerned about the birthparents' well-being, they solicit feedback from those who have gone through the process about how it can be improved. Just as importantly, they take the time to listen to them. Programs that are oriented to birthparents include them on their policy boards and committees.

Advocacy for birthparents can take a variety of forms. For reasons of shame, fear, or shyness, to mention a few, some birthparents are unable to effectively assert their interests. When this is the case, professionals may need to speak on their behalf. As prospective birthparents work out a master plan for the adoption with prospective adoptive parents, for example, it's essential that the birthfamily's wishes and expectations be expressed and built into the plan. If the birthparents turn timid or bashful, the professional can not passively sit back while an unbalanced plan takes shape. He or she must intervene and bring the birthparents back into the discussion.

In another vein, every adoption program needs an advocate who will champion the cause of birthparents as policies and procedures are established and revised. As pregnancy workers, they sometimes have less stature in their systems than their peers who work with adoptive parents, but they often do more than their colleagues to set the tone in a system. These champions for the cause of respectful treatment of birthparents are invaluable. Additionally, there are other times when professionals need to speak up to defend the general image of birthparents. Much of the work to improve the public's understanding of birthparents occurs in the course of business luncheons and backyard conversations with neighbors.

The Key to Enduring Inclusion: Well-Prepared Adoptive Parents

Once again, let me emphasize that adoptive parents are in no manner diminished when programs prioritize birthparents and identify with them. In fact, I'm convinced the opposite is true. Any program that is serious in its desire to serve birthparents is very conscious of the need to serve adoptive parents with great effectiveness.

Of all of the factors that characterize a birthparent-friendly program, none is more important than the resolve to fully prepare prospective adoptive parents for the journey. A program is only as good as its adoptive parents. Its hopes of making lasting room for birthparents can only go as far as adoptive parents take them. There is no greater gift to birthparents than to link them to well-nurtured and well-prepared adoptive parents, for these are the folks with whom they will interact through the years. Adoptive parents who understand the importance of keeping birthparents involved will exhibit the same attitudes we just considered in professionals. If they believe in birthparents, they will go out of their way to include them.

There's no way around the fact that birthparents are very dependent on the goodwill of adoptive parents. The most charming of birthparents will not get very far in their efforts to interact with adoptive parents who are fear-ridden and hold possessive attitudes about their adopted children. If, on the other hand, a system connects birthparents to adoptive parents who truly "get" the concepts of open adoption and are convinced that birthparents are of great and enduring importance to their children, it will have served all parties with respect.

To that end, I offer the following suggestions to help adoptive parents as they interact with their children's birthparents.

Friendly Pointers for Adoptive Parents Interacting with Birthparents

- ∾ Face your fears and insecurities and do your best to settle them. Do you fear the disapproval of your child's birthparents? Their grief? Their bond with their child? Work through these concerns so, instead of worrying about what could go wrong and operating defensively, you can relax, be yourselves, and enjoy the relationship.
- ∾ Create an atmosphere of inclusion and belonging. Warmly welcome them and leave no doubt about your sincerity. Bearing in mind the Golden Rule, do your very best to help them feel at home. Chances are great that the comfort of the relationship will be directly related to your success in creating a welcoming atmosphere.
- ∾ Go to them. Enter their space. Let the relationship be reciprocal and balanced. Let them teach you what they have to teach. Let the relationship involve more than adoption! Get out of the living room and have some fun exploring the interests you have in common. Otherwise you will drive each other crazy!

∽ Since your life circumstances may be more settled than theirs, operate as though the ball is always in your court. Take initiative to keep the relationship lively and current. Even if your efforts sometimes meet with little or no response, do your best to keep the connection alive because it holds great importance to your child. Resolve to make the relationship work, and be prepared to hold up your end and more if need be.

∽ Communicate frequently. Keep those cards and letters coming! Send lots of pictures, and be sure to include the cute ones. You may fret that you are "rubbing it in," but you are actually letting the birthfamily know that their hopes for their child are being realized. Take the time to keep them informed about significant matters. Your neighbors and colleagues at work may tire of hearing about this wonder child, but his birthfamily will always be glad to hear of his accomplishments. What's more, if you volunteer information, the birthfamily will feel no need to "pry" for information. When information flows easily, everyone benefits.

∽ Communicate clearly. Be very clear in your messages, and seek clarity in theirs. When you don't know what's going on with them, ask. Be careful not to presume too much. Double-check to be sure you are clear about their meaning, then check one more time. Resolve to always be honest with the birthfamily. Express concerns directly and graciously. Part ways with a clear plan for the when, where, who, and how of the next contact.

∾ Encourage a sense of teamwork, with an eye toward creating an exceptionally supportive circumstance for the youngster. This much-loved
child needs the affirmation of all the key people
in her life; she will surely benefit from the cooperative efforts of all of you.

∾ Respect them. Honor their need to control their
lives and their need for privacy. Let them be in
charge of their own story. Be careful not to pa-
tronize them. Take genuine interest in them
and care for them, but don't impose your ideas
as to how they should live.

∾ Defend their honor. Help the well-intended but
uninformed people you encounter to understand that the decision of your child's birthparents to entrust you with the responsibilities
of parenthood was anything but a statement of
disinterest in this remarkable child. Rather, it
was an indisputable act of love. It's okay to be
uncharacteristically ferocious about this if need
be, for it's a fine thing to defend the reputation of
a friend; in the process, you are helping to put
adoption on a more even keel.

∾ Remember Mother's Day and Father's Day.

Chapter 14

Pretty Much Regular People, Doing the Best They Can in Difficult Circumstances, Who Are of Great and Never-Ending Interest to Their Children

As we have seen, people have many opinions about birthparents. The fact that most people do not actually know much about birthparents means, unfortunately, that these opinions are frequently uninformed. Sadly, our review of perspectives on birthparents has shown that the preponderance of opinions are negative; it's difficult to find a fair-minded description of birthparents. Through the years, unfavorable images have ranged from the legendary "fallen woman" to the more contemporary assessment that they are dysfunctional. Lodged between these old and new viewpoints are several other unflattering takes on birthparents. Our exploration of the birthparent realm has touched on views that depict them as reckless risk takers, heartless taboo breakers, and fickle mind changers. A few particularly callous onlookers simply

223

see them as temporarily useful—biologically indispensable but psychologically expendable.

This assortment of perspectives covers a lot of ground, but none comes close to accurately describing birthparents. If these common slants miss the mark, how do we describe birthparents? Just who are these people, so long in the shadows, known as birthparents? Obviously, it's difficult to generalize about birthparents because they are an extraordinarily diverse group. None of our usual labels for describing people apply. I believe, however, that we can make a few observations about them that make sense most of the time.

Pretty Much Regular People...

The unspectacular truth is that most birthparents are rather ordinary people. Naturally, there are extremes in their ranks— some who are exceptionally effective and some who are unusually ineffective—but most birthparents are multi-dimensionally average. Just like our friends and neighbors, they present a complex mixture of strengths and weaknesses. Now and then, of course, they leave us shaking our heads in wonder, amazed they can be so wise and generous at one junction and so shortsighted and petty at another; but most of the time they are unremarkable, in the mainstream of life, getting by from day to day, and doing the best they can.

Doing the Best They Can...

Birthparents love their children and are serious about their responsibility to provide for their basic needs. Making this decision is a frightening responsibility, and it is to their credit that few take it lightly. Only the coldest of critics would suggest anything less than the idea that birthparents desperately want what is best for their children.

A mighty challenge, though, is packed into that small word *best*, and birthparents spend endless mental, emotional, and spiritual energy trying to figure out how it applies to their children. What is best? They know it is good and natural for children and parents to stay together, but they also know that children deserve security and opportunity. Since both views make sense to them, we can safely presume that they will feel great and lasting ambivalence about their experience. There will also be loneliness. Others can offer ideas, advice, and support, but the decision ultimately falls on the shoulders of each particular birthmother. In the end, "best" is for her to decide. It is a determination made through painstaking consideration of the many variables involved, not the least of which are her particular circumstances.

In Difficult Circumstances...

There's nothing easy about being a birthparent. Coming to terms with pregnancies that are awkward, untimely, or unsupported, their mettle is tested in every phase of the experience—making the decision, implementing it, and living with it over time. To the chagrin of those who wish to portray adoption as an entirely positive way to go, thoughtful birthparents describe their experience as a painful concession to necessity. It is an excruciating choice that is only made when external and internal circumstances require it. Even when the adoptions they fashion meet or exceed the expectations of everyone involved, birthparents find their satisfaction is tinged with sadness. Pleased as they may be that they have been able to make the best of very difficult circumstances and that their children are thriving, some resilient part of them wishes things could have been different.

...Of Great and Never-Ending Interest to Their Children

Lifegivers are important to their children throughout their children's lives. This is such a fundamental truth it almost seems foolish to state it so baldly, yet it needs to be said. Adopted children who feel permission from their adoptive parents to show interest in their birthfamilies clearly are interested in them. Even when birthparents present many liabilities, children find them interesting. It's difficult, after all, to be indifferent about one's origin.

Although critics of open adoption worry that involved birthparents will loom as alternative parents to the children and confuse them, we have seen none of that in our program at Catholic Human Services. Rather, involved birthparents represent "more" to a child—more information, more relationships, more opportunities, more love. The observation that birthparents are important to the children they entrusted to adoptive families is the cornerstone of open adoption. If we believe children benefit from interaction with their birthfamilies, we have little choice but to do all we can to find ways to keep birthparents involved.

Beyond Us and Them: The Normalization of Adoption

Perhaps touting the notion that birthparents are "pretty much regular people" seems silly, but I see the idea as nothing less than revolutionary in impact. This seemingly modest shift in perspective has the power to eliminate much of the we-they thinking that has divided the adoption community for so long. How liberating it is to discover, after decades of fearing another group, that "they" are an awful lot like "us." Commenting on the similarities between birthparents and adoptive parents, adoptive mother Carrie Kent puts it this way:

> I listen to and talk with adoptive parents all the time, both online and in person. I listen to their fears. I listen to their joys and their sadness. I listen to their pride in and love of their children. I also listen to and talk with birthparents all the time, and what do I hear from them? Joy, sadness, and pride in and love of their children. The barest of threads separates us. And yet so often that thread is made of steel. It is a thread of lies, deception, and fear.... How am I different from the first moms of my two children? Well, obviously, the thing that separates us is that they have had crisis pregnancies, and I have not. But does that really make us so different? Did I not have sex without the benefit of marriage? Did I at various points in my youth find love in all the wrong places? Let's be honest here.... Did I sometimes run chances and suffer fear for my actions?... So who am I to judge? It was not the stern abstinent character I was brought up to have been that saved me. It was, quite simply, luck.

If we can focus on similarities rather than differences, chances are good our interactions will be less driven by fear. Regular people, after all, seldom frighten us. While we worry about getting involved with "those kind of people," whoever those kind of people are, we feel comfortable and confident about interacting with ordinary folks and presume a spirit of reciprocity will be in effect. We hold reasonable expectations of regular people, neither too much nor too little. We know regular people aren't perfect, but by and large we find them quite reliable.

There is some hazard in advancing the idea that birth-parents are regular people. Regular people, after all, are dismissed as predictable, uninteresting, and unimportant a thousand times a day. It's a risk worth taking, however, for this wonderfully mundane appraisal is light years beyond their prior status as people who were considered different from and less than others. Perhaps we will know a better day has arrived when, instead of finding birthparents electrifying or terrifying, we confess that sometimes we find them a little on the unexciting side.

We have many reasons to seriously consider this idea that birthparents are pretty much regular people—not the least of which is that this is the way most birthparents think of themselves. Several birthparents did me the favor of previewing this manuscript. In studying their comments about it, I found they were the most excited about a statement in Chapter 2, where I wrote, "Most birthparents I know do not like being nominated for sainthood any more than they like being written off as uncaring persons. They know neither version is true. They simply hope for acceptance as normal persons struggling to do the best they can in extremely difficult circumstances." Acceptance as ordinary people does not seem like too much for them to ask of the rest of us.

If we can come to see that the world of adoption is inhabited by pretty much regular people, the institution can at last shed some of its artificiality and become less peculiar and anxious. Most people, after all, are far more relaxed when they know the people they are working with. We can deal with things when we know the who, what, where, when, and how of the matter, or when, as may be the case in some difficult circumstances, we know what we are up against. It's when we are dealing with something or someone unknowable that we get a little crazy. I believe the system's dogged determination to protect pretty much regular people from each other contains substantially more craziness than is found in the people it is fanatically protecting against.

My hope and prayer is that our effort to more fully understand birthparents will launch a spiral of acceptance. As we get to know them better, we will fear them less. As we fear them less, we will welcome them more heartily. If birthparents accept this welcome and join the adventure of ongoing adoptive relationships, many lives will be enriched.

Bibliography and References

The American Heritage Dictionary of the English Language (3rd ed.). (1992). Boston: Houghton Mifflin.

Arms, Suzanne. (1983). *To Love and Let Go*. New York: Alfred A. Knopf.

Burlingham-Brown, Barbara. (1998). *Why Didn't She Keep Me? Answers to the Question that Every Adopted Child Asks*. South Bend, IN: Diamond Communications.

Carter, Stephen L. (1998). *Civility: Manners, Morals, and the Etiquette of Democracy*. New York: Basic Books.

Dostoevsky, Fyodor. (1981). *Notes from the Underground*. New York: Bantam Books.

Dusky, Lorraine. (1979). *Birthmark*. New York: M. Evans and Company.

Franklin, Lynn, with Elizabeth Ferber. (1998). *May the Circle Be Unbroken: An Intimate Journey into the Heart of Adoption*. New York: Crown Publishing Group.

Gritter, James L. (1997). *The Spirit of Open Adoption*. Washington, DC: CWLA Press.

Grotevant, Harold, and McRoy, Ruth. (1998). *Openness in Adoption: Exploring Family Connections*. Thousand Oaks, CA: Sage Pubications.

Jackson, Rosie; Weldon, Fay; & Jackson, Rosemary. (1994). *Mothers Who Leave: Behind the Myth of Women Without Their Children*. London: Pandora.

Jones, Merry Bloch. (1993). *Birthmothers: Women Who Have Relinquished Babies for Adoption Tell Their Stories.* Chicago: Chicago Review Press.

Kent, Carrie. (1999, April). *Finding the Heart to Share.* Presented at the Seventh Biennial Open Adoption Conference, Traverse City, MI.

Landman, Janet. (1993). *Regret: The Persistence of the Possible.* New York: Oxford University Press.

Mason, Mary Martin. (1995). *Out of the Shadows: Birthfathers' Stories.* Edina, MN: O.J. Howard Publishing.

Melina, Lois Ruskai, and Roszia, Sharon Kaplan. (1993). *The Open Adoption Experience: A Complete Guide for Adoptive and Birth Families—From Making the Decision through the Child's Growing Years.* New York: HarperCollins.

Merriam-Webster's Collegiate Dictionary (10th ed.). (1997). Springfield, MA: Merriam-Webster.

Moorman, Margaret. (1996). *Waiting to Forget: A Mother Opens the Door to Her Secret Past.* New York: W.W. Norton & Company.

The New Lexicon Webster's Dictionary of the English Language. (1987). New York: Lexicon Publications.

Paskowicz, Patricia. (1982). *Absentee Mothers.* Totowa, NJ: Allanheld, Osmun.

Pavao, Joyce Maguire. (1998). *The Family of Adoption.* Boston: Beacon Press.

Peterson, Eugene H. (1992). *Under the Unpredictable Plant: An Exploration in Vocational Holiness.* Grand Rapids, MI: William B. Eerdmans.

Peterson, Eugene H. (1998). *The Wisdom of Each Other: A Conversation Between Spiritual Friends (Spiritual Directions).* Grand Rapids, MI: Zondervan Publishing House.

Pohl, Christine D. (1999). *Making Room: Recovering Hospitality as a Christian Tradition* Grand Rapids, MI: William B. Eerdmans.

Popenoe, David. (1996). *Life Without Father: Compelling New Evidence That Fatherhood and Marriage Are Indispensable for the Good of Children and Society.* New York: The Free Press.

Roles, Patricia E.. (1989). *Saying Goodbye to a Baby: Volume 1. The Birthparent's Guide to Loss and Grief in Adoption.* Washington D.C.: Child Welfare League of America.

Roles, Patricia E.. (1989). *Saying Goodbye to a Baby: Volume 2. A Counselor's Guide to Birthparent Loss and Grief in Adoption.* Washington D.C.: Child Welfare League of America.

Romanchik, Brenda. (1994). *A Birthmother's Book of Memories.* Ann Arbor, MI: R-Squared Press.

Ruddick, Sara. (1995). *Maternal Thinking: Toward a Politics of Peace.* Boston: Beacon Press.

Schaefer, Carol. (1991). *The Other Mother: A Woman's Love for the Child She Gave Up for Adoption.* New York: Soho Press.

Severson, Randolph W. (1994). *Adoption: Philosophy and Experience.* Dallas: House of Tomorrow Productions.

The Shorter Oxford English Dictionary (3rd ed. rev.). (1959). London: Oxford University Press.

Silber, Kathleen, and Speedlin, Phylis. (1982). *Dear Birthmother: Thank You For Our Baby.* San Antonio, TX: Corona Publishing.

Smedes, Lewis (1993). *Shame and Grace.* New York: HarperCollins.

Smith, Evelyn (Ed.). (1963). *Readings in Adoption.* New York: Philosophical Library.

Solinger, Rickie. (1992). *Wake Up Little Susie: Single Pregnancy and Race Before Roe V. Wade.* New York: Routledge.

Spelman, Elizabeth V. (1997). *Fruits of Sorrow: Framing Our Attention to Suffering.* Boston: Beacon Press.

Wadia-Ells, Susan. (Ed.). (1995). *The Adoption Reader: Birth Mothers, Adoptive Mothers, and Adopted Daughters Tell Their Stories.* Seattle: Seal Press.

Waldron, Jan L. (1995). *Giving Away Simone: A Memoir.* New York: Anchor Books.

Wells, Sue. (1994). *Within Me, Without Me. Adoption: An Open and Shut Case?* London: Scarlet Press.

Wilson, James Q. (1993). *The Moral Sense.* New York: The Free Press.

Wolff, Jana. (1997). *Secret Thoughts of an Adoptive Mother.* Kansas City, MO: Andrews & McMeel.

About the Author

James L. Gritter, MSW, is a child welfare supervisor and open adoption practitioner with Catholic Human Services, Traverse City, Michigan. He is the recipient of the Baron-Pannor Award for Outstanding Contributions in Open Adoption. His previous books include *Adoption Without Fear* (Corona, 1989), which he edited, and *The Spirit of Open Adoption* (CWLA Press, 1997). He and his wife have three daughters and live in Williamsburg, Michigan.